Ju Average Guy

PAUL JASON

Beaten Track
www.beatentrackpublishing.com

Just Your Average Guy

First published 2016 by Beaten Track Publishing
Copyright © 2016 Paul Jason

ISBN: 978 1 78645 069 2

Beaten Track Publishing,
Burscough, Lancashire.
www.beatentrackpublishing.com

Table of Contents

1. THE EARLY YEARS AND BEYOND............................ 1

   1–1 The Early Years...3

   1–2 Teenage Traumas...7

   1–3 Crossing the Line..13

   1–4 The Aftermath...18

   1–5 The Dawn of Full Dressing....................................22

   1–6 Rebellion...27

   1–7 Dawning of a New Era..32

2. THE FEARS 35

   2–1 Defence Mechanisms...37

   2–2 Narrow Escapes..44

   2–3 Fire Alarms and Sudden Death............................48

   2–4 Telephone Chatlines..50

   2–5 Burglary...53

   2–6 Holidays...56

   2–7 Television, Stress and Mini-Breakdowns..............66

   2–8 Public Reaction..69

   2–9 Potential For Being Exposed................................71

   2–10 To Tell or Not to Tell….....................................77

3. VENTURING OUT **81**

3–1 Craving Acceptance 83

3–2 From Angela to Manchester 85

3–3 Reconnaissance 89

3–4 Metamorphosis 93

3–5 Hello, World! 97

3–6 Making Allies 103

3–7 Logistics 109

3–8 Surveillance 116

4. TRYING TO MAKE SENSE OF IT ALL **117**

4–1 Cross-Dresser, Transvestite or…? 119

4–2 Fatherhood 122

4–3 Behaviour Management 129

4–4 Missed Opportunities 131

4–5 Why? 135

4–6 Perversions 147

4–7 Therapy 152

4–8 Time For a Little Controversy 161

AND FINALLY… **165**

About the Author **166**

1.
THE EARLY YEARS
AND BEYOND

1–1

The Early Years

The sun shone gloriously that fine day, as we sipped cups of tea in my grandmother's back garden. Well, in an attempt to be more precise, I was probably more likely to have been on dandelion and burdock back in those hazy, crazy, early 1970s days. Half a dozen or so of us were sitting there that afternoon – chatting, laughing and generally enjoying that great British rarity – a sunny summer's day. The sycamore trees in the garden next door, so often despised due to their imposing size, were, that day, offering us sanctuary by way of a dark and cooling shade. The occasional rustle of leaves in a welcoming breeze echoed around the garden like a therapeutic symphony. A chorus of birds chirped with content, blending with the distant sounds of an ice cream van, whose owner was no doubt enjoying what was sure to be a boost in the usual takings. Other sounds that are now deeply entrenched with images of summer could be heard all around us: children playing, shrieking and shouting with glee; lawnmowers being pushed across gardens with an enthusiasm not normally present on a cooler, cloudier day; a radio playing from a neighbouring garden at a volume that would not usually be tolerated. But hey, it was summer, the sun was shining and we were all going to make the most of it.

This scene is somewhat special for me, for it is my very first memory and I was four years old. Now, whether a memory that contains the song 'Chirpy Chirpy Cheep Cheep' is a good one or not remains to be seen. Maybe that is why I am so emotionally scarred today? I joke, of course, for I do like that song.

Although I didn't know it at the time, that day was incredibly important for me. It would prove to be the platform upon which the rest of my life would be built. And, despite the many highs, lows, disappointments and blows that have occurred along the way, that platform has remained solid throughout – whether I like it or not.

In an attempt to escape the afternoon heat, I decamped into my grandmother's front living room leaving other family members outside in the rear garden. The living room was much cooler and more shady than the rear of the house and thereby offered me a worthy retreat. I was a typical Briton in the making, complaining when we didn't see the sun but also looking for an escape route once it appeared. As I scanned the small room with its nicotine-tainted wallpaper and subsequent lingering aroma, my eyes fixed upon a basket beneath a table near the window. The basket contained a limited number of toys that were there for my amusement on days such as that. Whilst occupying my attention for a certain amount of time, I would usually tire of the toys after a few minutes and seek something else to grab my interest.

After a while, I was joined by a young and attractive family member called Jane, who sat near me on the sofa. Jane was my mother's cousin and would have been around twenty years old at the time. Having since seen photos of what she looked like in those days, I can certainly say that she was both stunning and gorgeous. With her black, bobbed haircut and dark mini dress, she was a definite carry-over from the 1960s.

Like me, Jane also felt the need to withdraw from the intensity of the afternoon sun. As I played on the floor with a toy car, no doubt making the usual 'brum brum' type of noise, Jane sat quietly nearby reading a newspaper. As kids tend to do, I swept the car up from the carpeted floor before crashing it down again accompanied by the inevitable screeching-of-brakes noise that I had perfected. Adults become magnets in situations such as these and it wasn't long before I was kneeling alongside Jane, wheeling the toy car along the arm of the couch beside her.

What happened next possibly changed the course of my life forever. It was to act as the blueprint upon which the rest of my days would be based. Within that tiny, darkened living room on that glorious summer's day, I became wired – programmed even – to take an avenue in life that most other boys would never dream of taking…but more of that later.

***

I was nothing special as a child. Being inoffensive, quiet and introverted meant that I hardly ever stood out from the crowd. The word 'average' seemed to be used in relation to me in more circumstances than I care to remember. It was a label that was permanently secured around my neck, stifling any potential for genius that may have been hidden away within the depths of my psyche. Instead of being nurtured and encouraged at school, any potential talent was suppressed – battered down by the immensity of the 'average stick', which was wielded with glee by my not-so-fantastic teachers. In truth, I was a bit of a dreamer, drifting my way through junior school and into high school without much of a strategy. And being honest further still, I was inclined to be somewhat lazy unless pushed, taking the easiest route whenever I could. I certainly had the ability, but I wasn't quite prepared to put in the time or effort when it came to schoolwork.

Like most boys of my age at the time, I adored the pop singer, Debbie Harry. I could gaze at her perfect facial features for hours. Her image was beautiful – so powerful, engaging and sexy. Though above all the female pop stars, film stars and other celebrities that were around at the time, my heart actually belonged to the television newsreader Anna Ford. I loved her dark bobbed hair, clean-cut image and well-spoken tones. She was cool, calm and professional in every sense. I wanted to marry Anna Ford. It was as simple as that.

Following on from the events of my first memory, a further significant event in my life unknowingly occurred when I was around twelve years of age. My grandmother had bought me a small ventriloquist's dummy for Christmas. It wasn't a proper one; it was more of a kid's toy, really. It had a plastic head and hands and a fabric body, but there was no filling inside the actual body part, making it somewhat limp in appearance. It had an opening at the back, within which to put your hand to operate its head and mouth. Whilst it was undoubtedly cheap in price and unarguably cheap in looks, I loved it all the same. My mother suggested stuffing it with kapok in order to pad it out, but I wasn't bothered; I was happy with it the way it was. That dummy went everywhere with me. I was very sentimental about things bought for me by people I loved. I adored Christmas – yes, because it meant I received presents, which, to a child, is very important – but more so because I loved the closeness of my family at such a magical time. Whilst I no longer believed in Father Christmas, the Christmas period remained exciting for me in many ways, even into adulthood, if I'm being honest.

On one particular occasion just prior to me turning thirteen, my sister and I stayed at our grandmother's house whilst our parents were out for the night. When my grandmother saw the ventriloquist's dummy, she also remarked that it could do with some padding inside it. I told her it was awaiting the addition of kapok filling, to which she replied that she would provide something to pad it out in the interim. She took the dummy with her out of the living room and returned soon afterwards, having packed some stuffing into it.

"That's better," she said, handing me back the dummy.

In fairness, it did look better for being a little more substantial. I so loved that dummy. I wish I still had it. I checked the attic recently, but alas it had gone. It was no longer anything more than a distant memory.

1–2

Teenage Traumas

By the time I reached thirteen years of age, I was undergoing the usual teenage traumas, with my emotions scattered all over the place. Puberty often left me feeling desolate with no one to turn to. I couldn't explain my feelings at the time, but it felt as though my body and emotions were being pushed and pulled in various directions. Each time I felt pushed one way, it seemed as though there were strong hands pulling me back in another. This all culminated one night into what I could only describe as being an 'inner bodily storm'.

My parents had invited their friends Don and Sally round to our house for drinks. They were great people and both had a fantastic sense of humour, though Don was much quieter than Sally. She had been very much overweight for many years and was, frankly, rather plain looking. But that aside, her personality was enormous and she was such a kind and friendly person. Her outgoing warmth was infectious and she made friends with people wherever she went.

However, I couldn't believe my eyes when I saw Sally that evening. She had lost so much weight and looked like a completely different person. A bright-red dress clung to the slender curves of her newfound slim figure. She now wore make-up, transforming her plain, usually subdued features into another dimension of attractiveness. As she walked into our living room, my jaw dropped in amazement. I noticed everything about her that was different, including her brown curly hair which was now pinned up instead of falling around her shoulders. Sally twirled to the compliments being paid by my parents, clearly enjoying the limelight afforded by her new image.

Wow! I thought.

I couldn't help but ogle her immaculate red dress. I noticed how it clung and stretched around her hips and upper thighs, how it enhanced her breasts, the swell of which could be seen above the V-shaped neckline. Her black nylons rasped as she crossed and uncrossed her legs, and when she removed her shoes, I could see her perfectly painted red nails through the toes of her stockings.

The sensation in my stomach amounted to combined feelings of tension and butterflies. An animalistic-type desire took hold of me. I wanted to run my hands all over her clothed body. Starting with her feet, I had the urge to move slowly up her nylon-covered legs and then onto her dress, caressing her amazing new figure through the flimsy, stretchy fabric. However, I was aware that I shouldn't be having such thoughts and felt terrible about having them. Sally was, after all, a family friend. I had never felt like that before and wasn't sure how to handle the situation. In my own mind, I had been naughty and let myself down badly. I was both ashamed and disgusted with my lewd behaviour. Nobody could ever get to know about the strange desire that had come over me from nowhere. I felt as though I had been possessed, as if someone or something had taken control of my usually stable mind.

During that same evening, I had also found myself strangely fixated on a picture of a young and extremely glamorous Danny La Rue, which was displayed in a TV schedules magazine. I was amazed at how a man could look so good as a woman. Dare I say it, I possibly had somewhat of a crush upon the image that he displayed, if not upon him himself. I didn't know was happening to me – first Sally and then a man in a frock – all on the same day.

I went to bed that night utterly confused. Lying there, I couldn't understand why I had felt that way. I wasn't sure whether it was Sally's new figure and general makeover that had attracted me, or was it actually the clothes themselves? Was it possibly a mixture of the two? She certainly looked stunning, and the clothes definitely enhanced her new image. As I continued to mull things over, it dawned on me that this wasn't actually the first time I had reacted in such a way. My mind flashed back to my earliest memory in my grandmother's house some nine years earlier.

***

Pushing that toy car along my grandmother's sofa, I naturally diverted it without a second thought so that it ran across Jane's legs. Wheeling it along the surface of her stockings, I suddenly and inexplicably found myself becoming fixated with her, so much so that I ended up discarding the toy. I was drawn to touch her legs – tentatively at first, checking out her reaction. When no chastisement followed, I pushed my luck. I was mesmerised by what she wore. Wanting to explore further, I began to pinch at the stockings. I was fascinated by the differing shades of black as I gently pulled them away from Jane's smooth legs. In an attempt to disguise my indiscretion, I recall saying, "Look, mountains," as the nylon formed tiny peaks between my finger and thumb. As I let the nylon go again, I was amazed to see it retreat instantly back to its original form. Suddenly, nothing else mattered that day. Someone could have brought the biggest, shiniest, noisiest toy of them all into the room but my attention remained fixed on the look and feel of those stockinged legs. I hadn't experienced such a thing before. It gripped me in a way that would affect my behaviour and lifestyle massively in years to come.

***

At four years of age, I could get away with such indiscretions. But as I lay in bed the night I had seen Sally, I puzzled as to why I had now, on at least two occasions, possibly been attracted to women because of the clothes that they were wearing. The clinginess and softness of those clothes certainly intrigued me. The stretchiness was also an attraction. The more I thought about it, the more perturbed I was by the realisation that my thoughts and desires in relation to Sally were not a one-off.

As for Danny La Rue, I didn't know what to think. Did I fancy Britain's biggest female impersonator of that time? If I was drawn to a man in a dress, could I actually have been bisexual and not have known it up until that point? In a similar way to Jane and Sally, I was unsure whether it was him that attracted me, or the thought of what he was actually wearing.

If I were confused at that point, things were about to get much worse because those thoughts and desires weren't merely going to melt away. A seed had been planted deeply within my mind, and I somehow needed to replicate the desires and emotions that I had felt earlier towards Sally. I adored the red dress that she had worn. I had also been captivated previously by the differing shades and stretchiness of Jane's stockings. I imagined the support and feeling of enclosure that such clingy clothing would bring to the body. Added to that, the fact that Danny La Rue looked so good in the photo, and the thought of a man being able to transform into a different, feminine guise, intrigued me to the core.

As such, I now needed to find out for sure what that feeling of support and enclosure was like. I was embarrassed to admit it, even to myself – and truly hated myself for it – but there was no way of denying the truth of the matter. I wanted to wear women's clothing. I had already experienced the look and feel of such items from the outside – whilst someone else was wearing them – but I now needed to feel the sensation by wearing such items myself.

Even though nobody else knew about my thoughts, the mere fact that I was having them had a negative effect upon on my behaviour. I became increasingly sheepish and withdrawn in my day-to-day demeanour. But if I *were* to try and wear women's clothing, my options in getting hold of such items were limited. There was no Internet in those days and besides, with me only being thirteen, I had no credit card or other means of paying remotely online. I also couldn't contemplate buying anything from a shop – even if I had the pocket money to do so.

After much thought, the only feasible option was to borrow something that belonged to my mother but the thought of that sent me spiralling into a depression with self-disgust. There was no way I could sink to such a depth, and it was so disrespectful to even think in such a way. I had already been irreverent in my thoughts towards Sally earlier that day and had been just as shameless to Jane years earlier. I was in a state of limbo, questioning my sexuality and sanity in entertaining such thoughts. How strange was I, wanting to wear an item of women's clothing? Needless to say, that night's sleep wasn't a good one. Above all else, I hoped that the strong desires that I had experienced throughout the day would have dissipated by the morning and I could once again get on with living my life as a normal teenage boy. I hoped that this was an inexplicable blip that may occur every nine or ten years before disappearing once again, just as quickly as it had arrived.

Waking the following morning, I was disappointed to find that my thoughts towards Sally the previous day had not been part of a bad dream. They *had* actually occurred, and I remained disgusted with myself. Thankfully, the urge to wear an item of women's clothing had disappeared or, at least, subdued significantly, for which I breathed a sigh of relief. This was, however, to be short-lived.

Later that day, the urge began to grow again. I became anxious, unsettled and unable to concentrate. The desire and its effects continued over the next few days, and I found myself in a vicious circle. I had the urge but could not quell or satisfy it, which led to me being frustrated, bordering on frantic.

Then it dawned on me. The answer had been there, lying before me all the time.

How on earth could I have been so dilatory?

1–3

Crossing the Line

I suddenly felt like Isaac Newton making a discovery. After all those days of angst and suffering, the solution had been right there in front of me. The ventriloquist's dummy had been within reach throughout, and potentially carried an extremely precious cargo. Although it didn't strike any chords at the actual time it happened, I was ninety-nine percent sure that my grandmother had put an old pair of tights into the dummy's back when she padded it out. I just had to find out, and my hands shook with trepidation as I brought the dummy out from my wardrobe.

As I sifted amongst the temporary padding, there indeed was a pair of nylon tights. Sitting there with them in front of me was like holding the key to a brand new, undiscovered world. Before me was a temptation that would take me to the 'dark side', but similarly, it would be the solution to end all my turmoil. But the relief of finding a solution was soon to be replaced by another concern. Whilst I now had what I wanted, those tights were my grandmother's. Although in effect she no longer wanted them and had given them to me, they were given for the sole purpose of helping to pad out the dummy. The last thing she would have considered was the thought that I would end up wearing them! I again felt it would be the ultimate disrespect to wear an item of a family member's clothing, and having beaten myself up with guilt, I put the tights back into the dummy, unworn.

Over the next couple of days, I was a little calmer in my demeanour because, despite still having the desire to wear that article of clothing, the thought that I possessed something 'in case of emergencies' provided me with a feeling of support. It also gave me time to think about the whole situation further.

Whether my first memory with Jane was the seed that started a life of cross-dressing, I remain unsure. Maybe that first memory was merely feeding into a fascination that was already there and had been formed and developed at some stage between birth and me turning four years old?

The truth is, I don't know and I am never likely to know. It is somewhat disturbing when you don't know why you do something or how and where it all began. It is as though you are not in control of your own mind. How do I begin to explain why, later in life, I developed an extremely strong desire to wear the clothing of the opposite sex? Many theories have been put forward but I don't think anyone really understands why there should be such a desire to cross-dress. After all, if I don't truly know my own reasons for doing what I do, how can I possibly expect anyone else to understand and, for that matter, accept or tolerate what I do?

As I contemplated my situation, my mind flashed back to my junior school years, and I was somewhat horrified when I realised that I'd had an inquisitive interest in ladies' clothing even then. The key factor being that, in those days, it was an interest as opposed a deep-set compulsion. I recall a Christmas play that was put on by the class a year senior to mine. At one point, there was a scene where a number of boys were playing the part of reindeer, pulling along Santa's sleigh. It was hardly a big-budget production. The reindeer costumes consisted of brown woollen hats with antlers; the boys wore brown t-shirts on their top halves and very little on their lower halves, save for their underwear and a brown pair of ladies' tights. However, I think the budget did extend to a blob of red paint on the end of Rudolf's nose.

I remember being mesmerised by how sleek and athletic those boys looked. It certainly wouldn't have had the same effect if they had worn jeans. The boys pranced onto the stage, raising their knees up high as though cantering. I was fascinated by how free and pronounced their movements were. And how, I wondered, did such a thin piece of material not tear under the pressure of being stretched so much? If I were being completely honest with myself, even at that stage, I also wanted to be one of those reindeer – and not because I wanted to wear the antlers…

The more I thought, the more it became clear that I had been interested in female clothing for a large part of my life. My feelings for Sally were, perhaps, just a culmination of everything that had gone before. It brought everything to the surface. My mind became tortured as the realisation set in that I may be in the process of becoming a transvestite. For a thirteen-year-old, this was a dark, confusing and frightening place to be. If I were ill or suffering problems at school, I could talk to my parents about it and they would automatically instigate an appropriate course of action. But what could I have done with this particular issue? There was no one for me to turn to and, therefore, I had no alternative but to suffer in silence.

The time eventually came when I could put off the inevitable no longer. My interest had become a compulsion, and I found that I could no longer relax or live my life effectively with such an urge lurking in the background. I had one or two false starts, whereby I had intended to wear the tights but then lost my nerve at the last minute. After all, this was a big deal. At thirteen, I was becoming a young man. My voice was breaking, and I was interested in girls, so I couldn't comprehend why I wanted to do this. Why was I standing behind a locked bathroom door with an item of women's clothing in my hand, contemplating whether or not to wear it? It was a lot to take in and that bathroom suddenly felt like the loneliest place on Earth.

I began to shake as I finally took the tights and slowly pulled them over my right leg. I was amazed at the softness of them as they clung to my skin. My heart was pounding to the point where I could hear my own pulse. My breathing was erratic as my body continued to shake with both fear and trepidation. Pulling on the second leg, I was amazed by the comfort that the tights brought. Pulling them up to my middle, I had finally done it. The magnitude of the relief and contentment had never before been experienced. It was as though an overbearing pressure had been lifted. I felt secure and supported, as though being hugged. Looking in the mirror, I discerned the different shades of the tights as they clung to the contours of my leg. All the time, I was petrified that someone would accidentally barge into the bathroom and catch me in the act. The embarrassment of being caught would have finished me. I knew for sure that I had locked and secured the door, but I still had to check it on at least three further occasions to appease my anxiety.

In pure contrast to the fearful pounding of my heart, there was also a sense of achievement. Having now fed the desire, I felt a wonderful sense of calm and contentment. Like a drug addict getting their fix, the fears, nerves and anxiety gave way to what became elation. On a total high, I was finally being true to myself. Little did I know it, but life would never be the same again.

I recall my attempts to justify my actions within my own mind. *I am not a transvestite; this is just something I need to do at this particular moment in my life, just something to get me by.* There was certainly some serious denial going on. After about five minutes, I removed the tights and put them back inside the dummy. This proved to be an ideal situation for me; the storage place for my secret was a legitimate one. If questions were asked as to why I was in possession of tights, I had the perfect alibi: my grandmother had put them in there. The fact that I had worn them myself would obviously have to remain hidden – until my dying day and beyond. Little did I know that this was just the beginning of what was to be a life of secrets and lies.

Following the elation, came an almighty crash. My actions affected me deeply. My family were downstairs and I now had to face them, knowing full well what I had done. The guilt that I felt, just like the high that had preceded it, was something I had never before experienced. Not only did I feel that I had let my family down, I believed that I had, in fact, betrayed them. I had been disloyal and disrespectful to them. My guilt was compounded by their unconditional love and care: the dedicated support, patience and time that they gave to me, without question or hesitation, on a day-to-day basis.

Another detrimental effect was that I now felt very much inferior to others, emasculated even; and whilst I already lacked confidence in many areas, what I had just done made me feel even more timid and insecure. My mind became tortured and I berated and taunted myself. I was disgusting and dirty. I was a pervert, a poof and a big girl; a let-down, a snake in the grass, a weirdo. But despite my self-put-downs, there was one thing above all else that I certainly was not…and that was a transvestite. Never. Not in a million years. No way was I a transvestite. Of that, I was adamant.

1–4

The Aftermath

I was uncomfortable with myself for the next couple of days and tried to come to terms with what I had done. I decided that I had no option but to try and put it all behind me. It was just something that I had to do in order to get it out of my system. Now that I had done it, I should let bygones be bygones, move on and treat the whole episode as being part of my character-building. I needed a new distraction – maybe a hobby to get interested in? Chess clubs were held at school; I could possibly join one of them? The plan to move on was strategically formulated within my mind. For good measure, and to end the silly escapade once and for all, I decided that I would rip the tights beyond recognition and cast them into the dustbin where they belonged. Situation sorted, normality resumed.

But there I was, later that evening, again standing in the locked bathroom, wearing the tights. I was mortified that I was unable to carry my plan of rectification through. As I stood there, I experienced exactly the same highs and lows that I had a couple of days previously. I was a nervous wreck, having to deal with such a wide spectrum of emotions within such a short space of time. Ultimately, having now succumbed to the dark side twice, I feared that I was embroiled in a situation from which there was no turning back.

In between my 'indiscretions', I still had a life to lead. There was school, which was approaching an important stage. I would soon be dropping certain subjects and undertaking others that may aid me in my career path. But away from the formalities, there were the basics to contend with: being able to look my family and friends in the eye, knowing full well what I was doing behind their backs. It was difficult. I felt shifty and untrustworthy. The meek and mild child that I had always been had become very much tarnished.

Such was the grip and control that my desire had upon me; I ended up wearing those old tights on many occasions thereafter. As days became weeks and weeks became months, the inevitable happened to what was a fairly delicate item of clothing; they became threadbare. The time had come whereby they were in such a state, with ladders and holes, that I had to think about disposing of them. But what would I do without them? Where would I get my next pair from? The truth was that I could no longer live and function properly without having easy access to this item of women's hosiery. The thought caused me much distress and panic.

Once again, I was in limbo. I had worn an article of female clothing and reached a level of ecstasy with the experience. I had learned that the mere wearing of this item could relieve my stress and induce an inner calmness and tranquillity. The only option open to me was the least favourable one. I would have to wait until my mother discarded an old pair of hers. I couldn't ignore this concept any longer; I knew it was wrong, both emotionally and morally, and it was hard for me to take. However, I was now addicted and badly needed my next fix. I tried to reassure myself that, as they would have been discarded, they were no longer my mother's; they would become mine. But as much as I tried to convince myself, the whole excuse was a bit thin.

One day, the opportunity was right there before me. Lying in a bin in my parents' bedroom was a pair of my mother's discarded tights. Now all I had to do was wait until they were transferred to the outside dustbin. I couldn't take them beforehand as it would be obvious that they were missing.

Rummaging around in the dustbin during the hours of darkness became a regular feature of my teenage years. On the night before the bins were collected, out I would sneak, searching frantically through a mass of potato peelings, newspapers and discarded food packets, desperately hoping I wouldn't be caught. It was dark where the bin was stored; very little in the way of street lighting aided me in my degrading actions. Recycling was not on the agenda back in those days, except in my case, where tights were concerned. As such, everything got thrown in the bin, and the more that was in there, the harder it could be to find my desired object.

The state of panic that I reached on some nights, when I was struggling to find the tights in the dustbin, was unbelievable. There is no exaggeration in my use of the word 'panic', either, because that was exactly what I felt. I had to find them at any cost because I couldn't be without them, and I didn't know when the next opportunity would be. I felt as though my world was closing in on me. My sanity depended on finding my secret stash, no matter how long it took. Once located, I would retrieve them and wash them in the bathroom sink. But then came the dilemma of drying them somewhere without anybody noticing. As a result, I had to develop levels of deviousness and secrecy pretty quickly in order to survive. I used to hang the drying tights out of sight on a coat hanger that hung in the gap between the bedroom wall and my mobile wardrobe. Drying them overnight also gave me eight hours where I was unlikely to be disturbed.

Once washed and dry, the retrieved tights needed to be hidden. But where could I hide them without being discovered? My deviousness had to sink to an even lower level. I took an empty talcum powder tin from my wardrobe.

I could store them in there, I thought.

My fear was, however, that my father may look in the wardrobe, wanting to borrow some of my talc. Feeling that there was something in the container, yet no talc coming out, he may then have opened the container out of intrigue and discovered the contents as a result. That would take some explaining. In an attempt to evade such an incident, I made a separator within the tin from a piece of card. Effectively, there was now an upper and lower level. I stored the tights in the lower level and kept a small amount of talc resting on the card in the upper level. As ingenious as it was, I no longer had easy access to them. It was just too messy and time-consuming to retrieve them for the idea to be practical.

The sad fact is that some drug dealers probably don't go to that level of deviousness, regardless of the potential retribution they may receive if caught. But despite me not doing anything unlawful and possessing only a mere piece of clothing, I felt I had no option but to sink to this level. This wasn't me being devious for the sake of it. It was an attempt not to upset and disappoint others. I had to hide what I was doing to protect those I loved, but I hated having to be so underhand with people who meant the world to me. If I could have been open without the potential for backlash then I would have been.

Eventually, I began to hide my reclamations from the dustbin within the wooden framework of my bed. A tear in the lower lining allowed me to conceal them within. This scenario of retrieving discarded tights from the dustbin, then washing, drying and hiding them continued throughout my teenage years. At the time, I wasn't interested in any other article, the reason being that pairs of tights would be discarded fairly regularly, so supply wasn't too much of an issue. Other clothing would likely be taken to the charity shop when no longer required, so there was no way I could retrieve it. Tights could also be hidden more easily, and being able to wear them under trousers allowed me longer periods of dressing and comfort without anybody else knowing.

1–5

The Dawn of Full Dressing

For the next two or three years, I was still in denial about being a transvestite. After all, I would never dream of dressing fully as a woman – not with wigs and make-up, in any case. Wearing ladies' tights was just something that I happened to do at that time. It brought me a sense of warmth and being. As for transvestites, I certainly couldn't contemplate for one minute being associated with them.

Despite trying to believe those thoughts, a few days after my sixteenth birthday, things took a major turn. A month away from taking my O' levels in school, the unthinkable occurred. My denial mechanism completely broke down, and I suddenly had an inexplicable urge to dress fully in female attire. I felt the same drive I'd had that first night a few years back when contemplating wearing the tights for the first time. For three years or so, I had been in denial about being a transvestite, but that was all about to change gloriously. Just like a thunderstorm that breaks several warm days in summer, reality was about to come crashing down upon me.

It was with some trepidation that I opened my mother's wardrobe when both my parents were at work. I had a free study day, but the only thing I was likely to be studying that day was the vast number of dresses, skirts and blouses that were hanging within that wardrobe. I perused the selection, picking out items for a closer look before finally settling on a black evening dress, black fake-fur coat, an old wig and some make-up. My hands shook as I nervously tried to apply the make-up to my face. The whole process was extremely rushed and, if the truth be known, I looked a mess. This was my first time and I was clueless. I probably looked more like a clown than anything vaguely resembling feminine, but this was the beginning of what was to be a steep learning curve for me. I squeezed my size-nine feet into a pair of high heels that were far too small and looked into the full-length bathroom mirror, surveying my new image. No matter how much I changed the angle, my slim boyish frame remained. I longed for the curves that Sally had displayed, and I wanted to experience the evening dress hugging them. Unfortunately, I just didn't have the figure to pull the image off satisfactorily.

My overall enjoyment of that moment was ruined by the fear that my parents might return home from work early and catch me in the act. Neither of them were due for a couple of hours, which should have allowed me a modicum of comfort, but the thought of being caught literally shook every bone in my body. Again, the excitement, elation and guilt all hit me at various stages during the period that I was dressed en femme that day. As with the first time I had worn the tights, my heart was pounding and my breathing was very much pronounced, the only difference being that I had now gone the whole hog and could no longer deny being a transvestite. I had to concede that this was what I was about. In many ways, it was a great relief because I felt as though I was finally free and no longer burdened with false denial. Admitting the truth to myself was a major pressure release in itself. Self-acceptance is an amazing thing, not just in this scenario, but in general.

I am a transvestite, I mused. It suddenly felt less painful to admit it.

In fact, it felt a little special. Being part of a minority group suddenly suited my semi-loner persona. To be dressed completely in women's clothing provided me with a warmth and security that comforted me immensely. I felt strangely mothered by the process. In many respects, the feminine side of me was identifying with the female populous, in a kind of swearing of allegiance with them. For the three-quarters of an hour or so whilst dressed, I was part of the sisterhood. Just as a football fan may show their allegiance by wearing their team colours, I, too, wore the kit that linked me to an image that I adored – that of femininity.

Even after the short time that I was dressed, the pressure of the situation was getting too much to bear. If my parents returned early, there would be no way that I would be able to remove all traces of make-up as well as returning the clothes to their rightful places without being caught. Such pressure meant that it was time to call it a day, though I could easily have stayed like that for hours. As I put my mother's clothes away, there was a certain amount of guilt but I was amazed that it was not worse. This was especially so, bearing in mind the magnitude of what I had just done. I had dressed as a woman and, in doing so, had stepped things up majorly. But the realisation and acceptance of both what and who I was soothed me enough to provide me with a safety net, preventing me from plummeting to the absolute depths.

Any guilt I was suffering was not so much because of what I had just done, but, more significantly, it was because it was my mother's clothing I had used in order to achieve it. I longed to be a few years older and have some money behind me, enabling me to have my own place and my own clothes. In my mind, I was crossing the line by invading somebody else's wardrobe and privacy – especially my mother's. Above all else, there was an additional concern. I was worried that I may not have put everything away exactly as I had found it. What excuse could I have given if an item was misplaced? The problem was, in all the excitement, I couldn't remember exactly where everything had been hanging prior to me removing it. This was despite believing that I had taken adequate notice of its positioning prior to its removal.

There had been a naughtiness in doing what I had done, and that in itself made the whole experience more exciting. Society dictated that I shouldn't be dressing that way, yet I was doing it all the same. It was a form of 'two fingers' to what I felt was a stuffy and restrictive culture. Dressing that way created a buzz…a high, but more than that, it provided me with an escape. Whilst my first venture into full cross-dressing wasn't great in terms of creating an image that I was pleased with, it still provided me with a different image – a transformation. I felt sure that seeing such a transformation in Sally a few years earlier, with her clingy clothes and attractively made-up face, inspired me to try and mirror that effect.

I had no confidence as a male, but a change of image to a more feminine façade calmed my inner tensions. The fact that I didn't look particularly good at that stage wasn't a major issue for me. It was more about me actually wearing the make-up as opposed to any effective enhancement it made. It was also more about me wearing a black evening dress and the satisfaction and contentment it brought, as opposed to whether it fitted me perfectly.

With all the clothes now put away, I returned to what I should have been doing in the first place – my O' level revision. My mother and father entered the house some time afterwards. My father joined me in the living room, looking stern.

"I don't want to hear of you doing that again," he said.

I immediately felt the blood rushing to my face. I could feel my whole face, neck and ears boiling under the pressure. *How on earth does he know?* I asked myself. The shock of what I thought was to come sent a blow directly to my solar plexus.

"Do what?" came my automatic, yet hesitant reply, awaiting the worst.

"Put the heating on," he replied.

My mind was a complete mess. Despite it being spring, the house had been cold, and I had put the central heating on to warm it up. That was a definite no-no in the daytime; for it was 1980s Britain, times were hard and money scarce. Central heating should not have been on in the day, especially in springtime. However, I took the telling off on this subject rather gladly, as, after all, I had expected far, far worse.

By now, I realised that I was on a road with no opportunity for turning back. Reality was muscling its way to the fore in that this was something strongly in-built within my character, something that I would have to live with for the rest of my life. As such, I wore items of my mother's and sister's clothing as much as I could thereafter. Full dressing, due to the complexity and the potential for being caught, was a rarity but the strong desire remained within me all the same.

1–6

Rebellion

Despite the acceptance of what I was, I still felt very much confused. Although I had been cross-dressing at a basic level for the last three years, I still struggled with the concept of stepping out of one persona and into another. Knowing what I had done and what I was as a person meant that I would tend to overcompensate when I was with my school friends. I felt a need, at sixteen, to be more rebellious. My mentality at the time was that if I was rebellious, then I was tough and hard, and – dare I say it – manly even. I was into punk and skinhead music and ended up getting into one or two situations that I shouldn't.

On one occasion, a friend and I pulled a large number of rocks out of a stone wall in a local park, scattering them across the footpath. Leaving the park that day, my conscience suddenly kicked in. I walked past some shops on the way home. There, within them, were honest traders doing a hard day's work, desperately trying to earn a living during hard times. And what had I done? I had vandalised a park wall. I felt terrible. Once again, I had let my parents and indeed myself down. Our incident made the headlines of the local paper, and for days afterwards, I agonised at the thought of the police calling at my address to arrest me. Being a rebel wasn't the true me. I hated it, but I was caught in a situation that I struggled to get out of at the time. All this was going on at the stage when I was meant to be studying. Instead, I spent those late-spring evenings in the local park, smoking cigarettes and drinking cheap cans of lager bought from an unscrupulous off-licence. To this day, I deeply regret my actions in that park. I loathe vandals and am ashamed to say that I was drawn to such acts myself at that vulnerable stage in my life.

My being constantly on the streets was an obvious concern to my parents. They pleaded with me to do some studying, but I wasn't interested. I recall the day I walked down our stairway in skin-tight jeans, 'bovver' boots and braces, and my father looked at me in despair.

"You're becoming a skinhead, aren't you?" he said.

The disappointment in his voice still echoes around my head today. However, if he had seen me walk down the stairs en femme as I had done previously, he would really have had cause for concern. Skinhead fashion would have seemed like an evening suit and tuxedo compared to that.

It was during this stage that I fell out with the police. I had been stopped by them on a number of occasions and been accused of things that I hadn't done. I felt that the attitude of the officers who had dealt with me was awful. However, being no angel at the time, I had to take the rough with the smooth. For everything I got away with, I got hassled for something I hadn't done. With the passing of time, I realised that things you believe are funny in your younger years are a complete nuisance in reality and, in certain circumstances, can have people living in fear. We never took things to that extreme; it was the usual pranks of ringing doorbells before making off, setting off air bombs late at night and taking gates from someone's house and putting them in the next-door garden. I was a pain, but for some reason used this façade as a kind of solstice from my newfound feminine alter ego.

The immaturity certainly didn't help in attracting a girlfriend. It also didn't help my confidence in having a little devil in my mind saying, 'What girl would want to be with you, anyway, a boy who wears girls' clothing?'

On one particular evening, though, as teenagers, we did think our luck was in. Two girls shouted something to my friend and me from the other side of the road. They were all smiles and tease. As they walked away, they kept looking back at us in a giggly, naughty sort of way. My friend suggested that we should follow them, to which I put up no argument. As we slowly strolled behind them, they continued to look behind, smiling all the way. They were a fair way ahead of us and were heading in the direction of the local park. Each time they turned a corner out of our sight, they stopped, allowing us to catch up a little. When they saw that we were still following, they continued on their way, eventually strolling into the park itself.

As we followed them through the gates, we saw that they were no longer on their own. They were standing with a dozen or so male youths. Both girls were still smiling back at us in a 'gotcha' type of way. The group were quiet, standing still and watching our every move, having probably been briefed by the 'honey trap' as they awaited our arrival. I didn't recognise the gang as being locals and fully expected a beating. Thankfully, nothing more came of it. We merely skulked away with our tails between our legs. But once again, I had been conned by girls. It was an all too familiar story. Most of my dealings with them seemed to end with them playing with my emotions. There was nothing in the park girls' behaviour that suggested they weren't interested or didn't want us to follow them. They appeared to be encouraging us. But all the time they were just toying with us. All I wanted was some female company and attention, but I just didn't know where I was when it came to girls. How was I meant to read the signals that they were giving me? The whole thing didn't make sense.

In many respects, it made me want to indulge in cross-dressing all the more. At least then I had access to a feminine persona that wouldn't cheat on me or lead me on and would be available when I wanted 'her' to be – opportunities allowing, of course. But the more I dressed, the more I became confused as to my expected sexuality. I still fancied girls, in spite of them being teases, but couldn't understand how I could be straight when I was compelled to dress fully as a woman.

It goes without saying that I failed most of my O' levels miserably. There was too much going on in my mind, too many distractions. Put simply, I didn't want to be sitting with my head in a book when I could be out drinking a can of lager and causing mischief in the park. Needless to say, the distraction of needing to cross-dress didn't help, either. Yet, I returned again to my schooling later that year in order to try and gain more qualifications. I knew obtaining qualifications was the way forward to a better life but just couldn't find the motivation or momentum to study. At seventeen, I scraped a few more qualifications, more by luck than judgement, because I again idled away my time in the local park and streets as opposed to settling down to study. However, I was less rebellious by that time, and with formal education finally behind me, things were about to become increasingly tough.

The 1980s saw harsh times that affected many in a detrimental way. Unemployment was rife, with many people struggling to find work. There was no reason why I would be an exception to the rule. Not feeling ready for an exhausting search for such work, I enrolled on an art and design course at a local college. It was to prove a big mistake, as nine months later, I was booted off for being a poor student. As a result, I found myself joining three million others in a period of unemployment. Long hours on my own, sitting in my parents' house, awaiting the delivery of my next supplementary benefit cheque, at least allowed me a little more freedom to dress as I pleased. But unbeknown to me, I was also beginning to develop a fear of leaving the house. I was spending too long cooped up inside and had lost all confidence in dealing with people on the outside. I was secure in my own bedroom. No one was going to hurt me or bother me whilst I was in there. Thankfully, I just about managed to snap out of it, but I was extremely self-conscious when I did manage to venture out. I felt as though the whole world was watching me, ridiculing me and waiting for me to fall flat on my face. However, I managed to reverse the situation at just the right moment. Another six months of staying in may well have allowed an agoraphobic grip to completely take over.

I timidly enrolled on a training programme to learn general building skills at the age of nineteen, and twelve months later, I was labouring for a local builder. I was hardly setting the world alight, but at least I was earning a wage and picking up some skills along the way. I was still living at home at the time, and despite earning a little bit of money, I continued to resort to wearing bits of cast-off clothing from my mother and sister. I longed to have access to my own items; I just didn't have the confidence to go into a shop and buy them for myself. Then, one December evening, something occurred that would lead me into a whole new chapter in my cross-dressing life.

1–7

Dawning of a New Era

One December evening, my mother asked me what I was intending to buy my sister for a Christmas present.

"I don't know," came my usual uninterested reply.

"She wants a camisole," my mother said.

The idea of looking through women's underclothing in a store freaked me out. I suppose it was mainly because of my own guilty mind. As such, I could have asked my mother to pick something up on my behalf, but it never came to the forefront of my mind. My thoughts were hijacked by the uncomfortable situation that prospectively lay ahead of me. Surely I would go bright red looking through the lingerie section of a department store? If I didn't at that stage then I definitely would when I took the item to the checkout. Expecting the sales assistant to be wondering whether the camisole was for me, my guilty mind would surely ensure that I would go bright red. However, I knew I had to overcome my fears otherwise my sister wouldn't get the present that she wanted.

As I was building myself up to the challenge of buying such an item, a thought suddenly hit me, and everything turned much, much brighter. There was a new dawning: if I felt so embarrassed buying a legitimate present for my sister then I may as well feel the same way about buying something for myself.

So there I was, amongst the fairy lights and tinsel, with a camisole for my sister in my hand. Trying my best to keep calm, I approached the hosiery section with the intention of buying something for myself. Nervously and ever so self-consciously, I grabbed the first pack of tights I came to, spending no time in looking at the size or colour as I did so. As I waited in the queue for the till, I hoped nobody walked by that I knew. With the camisole, I had a valid excuse; however, if somebody asked me who the tights were for, I could have been in trouble. After all, if I said they were all for my sister, they may have approached her at a later stage saying, 'We saw Paul buying you the camisole and tights at Christmas.' Upon hearing that, my sister would surely have thought, 'What tights?' Whilst there was only a slim chance of such a conversation actually occurring, it still caused me concern all the same.

I did go somewhat red whilst being served. I know that. I felt my face, neck and ears heat up immensely. But having bought the items, I had now entered a new era. No more would I be rummaging through dustbins in the night as though I were a desperate tramp. No more would I have to feel guilty about wearing female family members' items. That was finally all behind me. If I had bought something for myself once then I could do it all again, and again. Christmas was always going to be the best time for me as so many men buy women's clothing as presents anyway. I would, therefore, merely blend in with the rest of the crowd at that time of year.

A new door had been opened, and the trainee transvestite was rapidly becoming a pro. One thing I was sure of, though: there would be no way back to the life that I once knew, not after discovering the ability to buy my own items and with so many years of dressing having gone before. Like it or not, this was to be my life…and I had to get used to it.

Soon after, I joined an agency, and at twenty-three, I found myself labouring on various building projects in London. Despite being extremely close to my family, I had fancied a change of scenery for some time and felt that moving away from home would be the making of me. There was plenty of work around at the time, especially in and around the Canary Wharf development and along the side of the River Thames where converting old warehouses into apartments was suddenly en vogue.

The building trade wasn't for me, though; I knew that from the start. It would do in the short term during my younger years, but I didn't fancy the thought of it in later life. Besides, it was all too macho for me. I would have felt far more at home as a hairdresser.

The first couple of years in the London building trade were nonstop; manic even. I was in a tiny hostel room with a bed, a sink and a wooden chair. Three hangers were on a rail protruding from the wall. As such, I didn't mind being out of the room and worked most hours to put some money aside. So long as I could make the last hour in the pub and at least had Sundays off, I was happy enough. After a while, I managed to get enough money together to put a deposit down on a small terraced house. House prices had dropped in parts of London in the early 1990s, making them far more affordable than they are today. My heart still belonged in The North, however, and I knew that I would return there again one day. However, now with money, independence and a place of my own, cross-dressing was to become an extremely significant part of my routine. I finally had the opportunity to indulge in a less guilt-ridden lifestyle, whenever the urge took a hold of me, which, usually, was more often than not.

2.
THE FEARS

2–1

Defence Mechanisms

Life can be lonely for a cross-dresser, not to mention fearful. Sometimes, I would finish work on a Friday evening, close my front door, and that would be it. I would have no further contact with the outside world until I reopened the door to return to work the following Monday morning. I would sustain myself with a diet of ready-made convenience food, cigarettes and, of course, alcohol.

Having moved away from the bosom of my family and the area in which I had lived all my life, I suddenly found myself in an unfamiliar place with no friends. Being quiet and introverted, I found it very difficult to establish myself amongst others. Yes, I had acquaintances and colleagues, but friends were, for the main part, absent. As such, the days when I wasn't at work could be long, and being stuck on my own drove me stir crazy at times.

Whilst I liked my own company and the resultant peace and quiet, those days were just too much. I knew that I should be joining social clubs or getting involved with charitable events to get me out of the house and at least increase my chances of meeting new people. I can't even deny that I knew that those options were open to me at the time. But still, I stayed alone, cooped up within the four walls of my house. Being as homesick as I was, and hoping one day to return back up north, only hindered my situation. It meant that, in reality, I shouldn't get too emotionally attached to anyone whilst based in London, for

I knew I would only have to prise myself away from that person somewhere down the line, causing much hurt in the process.

Not that I didn't try for romance whilst based down south, because I did. I am only human, after all. I suppose the ideal would have been to have met that special person and take them back up north with me. The reality was, however, that if I did meet someone from the south, I would likely have been the one required to settle down there with them. For all the negatives and mixed emotions that surrounded me at the time, what my situation did present was an ideal opportunity to dress en femme as and when I pleased. Nobody was likely to call and disturb me during those long lonely days.

However, the fear of being discovered or caught in the act while dressing is a fear that has blighted me since I very first started. I would regularly suffer nightmares about being stranded outside whilst dressed in female attire and the ensuing embarrassment and humiliation that such an experience would bring. Therefore, even in a supposed relaxed state of mind – i.e. whilst sleeping – the ultimate fear of discovery reigned supreme. I quickly learned that there was no escape from the fear of being outed. The majority of cross-dressers tend to be non-scene, meaning they don't go out dressed or take part in the cross-dressing scene in an active way. Most don't have the confidence, opportunity or perhaps inclination to go out and meet others of a similar standing. For those content not to do so, fine. For others, it may be a desire that will have to be suppressed for a lifetime, no matter what consequences it may have on their long-term psychological well-being.

Away from a lack of opportunity, the main restriction will be the underlying fear of discovery and retribution that such discovery may bring. The potential for losing your family, your job and your dignity are all extremely high prices to pay for a little indulgence, and the thoughts of such penalties weigh heavily on the mind. The word 'indulgence' is used slightly tongue-in-cheek because this isn't about having that extra cream cake following a bad day at the office; it's about the need to feed a driving, long-standing and deep-set compulsion.

From an early age, I began building and adapting defence mechanisms in order to avoid or lessen the chance of being discovered. I have already referred to the creeping around antics that I had to adopt as a teenager. In truth, it was always about being one step ahead of the rest. But the fear of discovery was always there, constantly clinging to me with a stubborn reluctance to being shaken off.

Closing the front door on those Friday evenings gave me a choice. I had moved to London, the great capital city of England with its bright lights and hustle and bustle. Maybe I could have gone to the West End and taken in the atmosphere? Perhaps I could have booked tickets for the theatre or become a little cultured by taking in a ballet? Maybe I should have gone to an art gallery or museum?

For all the choices that lay before me in that great city, I still closed the door to life on the outside. As tempting as those options were, the key was turned in the lock and the bolt and chain were secured into position. The draw of being able to relax as my alter ego was just too strong. If I could have been in two places at once, it would have been great. However, this was the real world, and I could only do one thing at a time.

With the option of finally being able to cross-dress unhindered and undisturbed, all other activities naturally paled into insignificance. The West End would have to wait until another day.

But why did I secure my front door as I did so early on a Friday evening? After all, the house was occupied. It wasn't as though I was leaving it unattended for the night.

The answer is simple. It was in case there was an attempted break-in whilst I was within the house, dressed. Obviously, any perpetrator would be unlikely to know that the house was occupied for them to attempt a break-in in the first place. However, without putting such security in place, it would only have taken a single kick for an undesirable to gain access through my closed door. With the locks engaged, they could still gain entry but it may have taken an extra two or three kicks. The importance here is that bolting my door would 'buy' me that extra second or two, during which I could shout and holler from upstairs, in an attempt to scare them off. Upon hearing that the house was occupied, it would hopefully deter them before they actually entered and confronted me whilst I was dressed. In my mind, it was crucial to think ahead and see the bigger picture. But sadly, that's how it always was for me. I was always concentrating upon the minutiae and therefore couldn't truly relax – even in the comfort and privacy of my own home. Such was my fear of being caught out.

I was somewhat paranoid, I suppose, but society had conditioned me to be like that. On those Friday evenings, my wardrobe of slinky, clingy fabric became my comfort zone, my guilty retreat. My feminine alter ego became an instant friend and confidante – non-judgemental, undemanding and faithful. I looked forward to seeing it and spending time with it. I would spend hours looking into my second self's made-up eyes, framed by painstakingly plucked and arched eyebrows. I missed it when it wasn't there, and in those times of absence, suddenly, I was alone again – very alone.

There were drawbacks to this kind of lifestyle, of course. Summer days would be spent locked away like a recluse. Curtains would remain tightly drawn even though the sun may have been shining brightly outside. I recall one of those summer days when neighbours were throwing garden parties with friends and the aroma of barbecues drifted through my open windows. Hearing laughter and frivolity, I recall sneaking the occasional peep through the gap in my closed curtains into next door's rear garden.

Seeing my neighbours and their friends having such fun, splashing water at each other, drinking and enjoying the warm sunshine, made me think. They were young and at that moment, appeared carefree. They were around my age and all looked content as loving couples. As I closed the gap in my curtains and turned around to face my darkened room, I took in the surroundings of my somewhat gloomy hideaway.

What am I doing? I wondered in despair. *What on earth has happened to me?*

I was a big boy now, though. A strangely dressed boy, maybe, but a big one all the same. It was my choice to do what I was doing – locking myself away instead of getting out there in the sun and making a life for myself. After all, no one was forcing me to stay in. *But,* was it actually my choice to do what I was doing? I was, to all intents and purposes, feeding a need, a compulsion. The compulsion hadn't been my choice. That just happened to be there from the very start. As for locking myself away on such a fine day, well it was society that dictated that. It was not me who opted for being banished under house arrest when dressed that way.

To demonstrate the hold that my need to dress had upon me, I recall an occasion whereby I had just dressed en femme one Friday evening. I had finished a long, hard day at work and was looking forward to a relaxed evening in front of the television. I was hungry – starving even – and upon opening my refrigerator, I found that I had no food within. A rapidly browning lettuce and a bottle of wine were all that greeted me. I had two choices; get dressed back into my male guise and go shopping or remain as I was and have nothing. I couldn't order a pizza or takeaway as that would mean greeting the delivery driver at my front door whilst en femme.

I thereby faced a potential dilemma. However, given the choice of feeding myself after a long, hard day or spending the evening dressed was a no-brainer for me – I chose the en femme option. Making such a choice clearly demonstrated the pull that cross-dressing had upon me. It took over my life and basic, yet important, requirements such as eating, were shoved out of the way. In addition, having seen the bottle of wine, there was no way I was able to leave that alone. When my stomach was empty, the more alcohol I wanted to drink. And the more I drank on an empty stomach, the more likely I was to be damaging my health.

Ringing telephones would remain unanswered when I was dressed – and for a very good reason. As I have already explained, I always tried to think one step ahead and had assessed such events as part of my defence mechanism by imagining the following type of scenario…

Having spent over an hour getting ready, with the make-up and jewellery meticulously applied – I am dressed to the nines. However, Cinders isn't going to the ball tonight. The landline phone rings. What do I do? Answer it or leave it? It may be important. It may be a family member who is in trouble or ill. But if I were to answer it, the worst case that could occur could be something similar to this:

> *Hi, Paul, it's Steve and Clare (friends from up north).*
> *How are you doing?*

To which I reply:

> *Hi, Steve, long time, no hear. I'm not too bad, how are*
> *you?*
>
> *Great, thanks. Anyway, surprise, surprise, we're in*
> *London, so we thought we'd pay you a visit, and guess*
> *what? Look out of your window. We are outside your*
> *place – right now! Put the kettle on!*

How would I get out of that one? I would literally have seconds to remove all traces of make-up, jewellery and clothing. Not to mention being able to compose myself following such a shock. Having answered the landline, they would know for sure that I was inside the house. If I'd answered on a mobile phone, I could have been anywhere, but in answering the landline, I would have been cornered in the house.

Even using a mobile telephone could still create problems as the following scenario demonstrates...

> *Hi, Paul, it's Graham. Where are you?*
>
> *Hi, Graham. I'm er...in The Red Lion.*
>
> *You're in The Red Lion?*
>
> *Yes.*
>
> *Funnily enough, so am I. Whereabouts are you? I can't see you.*
>
> *Sorry, I meant The Black Bull; yes, I'm in The Black Bull.*

That is the problem with lying. It is so easy to get caught out. Especially when you have to make things up on the spot and start thinking on your feet. I was always useless at that. I could never have been a wide boy, even if I had wanted to be. I never had the patter to get out of tricky situations easily. One lie very often leads to another, which, in turn, leads to another. Hence, my reason for leaving telephones well alone when dressed.

Over the years, I relied heavily on the excuse of being in the bathroom to get me out of a potentially tricky situation.

> *Why didn't you answer your door?*
>
> *Sorry, I was otherwise engaged in the bathroom.*

Unbeknown to me, my life had become one long scenario of living on the edge. I lied, I cheated, I ducked and I dived. Somewhere, somehow, I found myself way off course. I was a million miles from where I wanted to be.

2–2

Narrow Escapes

I was nearly caught out one day, whilst dressed en femme at my parents' house. This was as a result of an unexpected visit by my sister. At the time, she lived around the corner, and I took the opportunity to dress, knowing that my parents were out for the afternoon. They weren't expected back for a good few hours, so it was a golden opportunity for me to escape into my feminine persona. Without warning, I heard the clinking of keys in the front door. The shock that gripped me sent an immense pain shooting through my body, as if I had been winded by a massive blow.

Naturally, I headed for the bathroom, clomping ungracefully with panic in three-inch heels as I went. My senses and coordination were shattered as a result of the shock. This was apparent by my slamming of the bathroom door instead of merely closing it. I turned on the shower, ripping off my clothes and stumbling about in the absolute mayhem of the situation. Diving into the shower, I rubbed my face vigorously with soap, desperate to get rid of all traces of make-up. There was no time for make-up remover in a situation like that.

My behaviour must have seemed very strange to my sister. If I heard her entering the house when in my male guise, then ordinarily, I would have walked downstairs to greet her before I took a shower. I decided, whilst in the shower, that I would blame my lack of greeting on the fact that I was wearing headphones at the time and, as a result, didn't hear my sister entering the house.

However, importantly, a bathroom had once again come to my rescue. I had sought sanctuary within them on many occasions when in fear of being caught dressed.

There are many different fears that stem from what I do. Removing all traces of evidence associated with having just dressed being one of them. There is the fear of opening the front door all macho and brimming with confidence and then realising that a diamanté earring has been left dangling from my earlobe.

On a number of occasions in the past, following a period of being dressed, people have said to me, *you look like you are wearing eyeliner*, or *you're very dark around the eyes, like you're wearing make-up*. In those days, I didn't have access to make-up remover as I couldn't bring myself to buy it. I therefore had to make do with soap and water, but that didn't always prove effective. In my failure to adequately remove all eye make-up, I aroused comment and possibly suspicion. Survival skills had to kick in again as I desperately attempted to save my dignity.

I, er...didn't sleep well last night; it must be down to that.

It doesn't matter how good or meticulous you are, either. You can clear up with military precision, removing all items from the scene, yet still risk getting caught. One particular occasion remains firmly in my mind. I had spent an hour or so dressing one afternoon when I lived in a bedsit up north. When I had finished, I carefully removed all traces of make-up and jewellery and put every last piece of clothing and associated items away. I had showered and was drying my hair when there was a knock on my door. Confident that I had hidden everything, I opened the door despite wearing no more than a pair of jeans. It was my neighbour, Mick, from the flatlet downstairs: a rough, tough man – an ex-army squaddie. We had always got on well and had spoken on several occasions previously. His bedsit was directly beneath mine and situated next to the front entrance into the main building in which we were based. It was clear that he was taking no chances. On a visit into his flat one day, I noticed an array of sticks, baseball bats and other clubs. All were lined up and accessible by his front door. He was certainly not one to be messed with and for some reason believed he was vulnerable to attack.

He was with me for twenty minutes or so, chatting, as we both put the world to rights. It was only after he had left the flat that I realised, with horror, my glaring mistake. I looked down at my bare chest to see the red indentations where I had been wearing underwired bra cups. My heart sank as I saw my man boobs highlighted like flaring beacons within the mirror. The marks were most obvious and what made it worse was if they were *that* obvious then, how prominent were they twenty minutes earlier when I opened the door to him? They had to have been even more obvious at that point.

I turned and looked at my back in the mirror. I saw the bra-strap indentation just as obviously etched across my shoulder blades and started to panic as my mind raced with questions. Would Mick have noticed? Surely he must have? But as a man and not being switched on along those lines, maybe he saw the indentations but the cause of them didn't register with him? I decided that if I were ever to be confronted on the subject, I would have to use the excuse of having a bad back and explain that the marks were due to me wearing a back support. Flimsy, I know, but it was the best that I could come up with. Fears such as this hound me all the time. I had been meticulous in clearing everything away but clearly wasn't attuned to the wider picture. Ninety-nine times out of a hundred, I would have put a shirt on before answering the door to someone. I am a private person and therefore don't do half-naked gladly – especially to relative strangers. I was stupid to have done so on that occasion. I was caught off guard, and it could easily have backfired.

What was even more annoying was that I didn't normally wear a bra. I didn't falsify any feature that I haven't naturally got. Examples here would include corsets, hip and bottom pads and false breasts, all of which are readily marketed to cross-dressers to enhance their figures.

My need to replicate the image of a woman didn't extend to body parts; it was purely related to the surface – the make-up, the wigs and the clothes. Therefore, if I were not using false breasts and had no natural breasts of my own, I had no need for a bra, either. Simple as that. I am a man, not a woman, and I never try to be like a woman in shape. I merely adopt a feminine image via the clothes and make-up that I wear. That is why I was so annoyed at letting myself down on that occasion.

Mick meant well, but he could be a bit of a pain. He had a habit of always calling round the very minute that I had dressed en femme. When I was in male attire, I wouldn't see or hear from him for days, but just as I was applying that final bit of make-up, there would be a knock on the door.

"Paul, are you in?" I would hear him shout.

I would freeze to the spot for what seemed like an eternity, eagerly awaiting the welcome sounds of his feet stomping back down the stairs. But it would ruin the potential for me relaxing properly. Being a bedsit, my front door led straight into my living room and sleeping area. Hearing my television from outside the door was easy. Plus, with him living below, he could hear me clomping about upstairs, especially when in heels. He, therefore, always knew that I was in but wasn't answering my door. Time to use the bathroom excuse again. This was a completely different scenario to when I had my own house in London. Despite certain fears, the freedom that I actually had to move around unhindered down there was amazing. But everything felt flimsy in the bedsit. I felt vulnerable and exposed.

2–3

Fire Alarms and Sudden Death

Hotels have always provided me with a good opportunity to dress in the past. This was especially so during periods when I was unable to do so at home. An overnight stay in a hotel, whilst on business or away on a course, was always enthusiastically accepted by me in order to provide a brief window of opportunity for freedom. But once fully dressed within the confines of the hotel room, the worries would still be there, niggling away at the back of my mind. For example, I was often more than a little anxious about what I would do in the event of the hotel fire alarm being raised.

How long would it take me to remove all traces of my female persona and make it to the fire rendezvous point? I have seen a couple of buildings go up in flames in my time and I know they can go up pretty quickly. I remember seeing a school on fire in London. It was very frightening. The speed at which the fire took hold of the building was incredible. Every so often, the wind would change direction and blow the black, toxic smoke back towards me and other onlookers. We had to quickly dive behind a wall to take shelter when we saw it coming. Despite us being outdoors and a fair distance from the fire itself, the smoke was still so black and choking that it would have damaged us if we had remained where we were.

With all that in mind, I have often considered what I would do with the hotel fire alarm scenario? Would I vacate the room as I was, thinking that the embarrassment of leaving the building en femme would be worth it in order to save my life? Or was there the possibility that I may vacate the room dressed, only to find it was a false alarm? It is this type of daily fear that means I can never totally relax as a cross-dresser, even when I'm away on business with little chance of people that I know knocking on my door.

One of my main fears, as morbid as it sounds, is dying suddenly. I fear that if I were to suddenly collapse and die then I would have no time to sort my affairs.

If I were told that I had four hours to live then I would take every shred of evidence regarding my cross-dressing to the local tip. This is put forward as an example, of course, for if I were actually given four hours to live, I would undoubtedly be in no fit state to make it to the tip! But you can spend years hiding your secret away to then die suddenly and have wives, partners or family members discover your secret life, hidden in car boots, secret compartments or office lockers. Granted, if I did die without sorting my 'affairs', I would no longer be around to be hurt by those events and disclosures.

The thing I have agonised over, though, is that my memory may be darkened, and my family, friends and loved ones would still have to live with the humiliation and potential backlash. I couldn't bear having my memory tarnished in that way and would hate to cause so much hurt without being able to explain the situation and try and make amends. I want my family and friends to remember me with pride, not to be burdened with gathering and disposing of the other side of me – the side that they didn't know when I was alive. Death is inevitable. One just hopes that when it comes, one can leave this world with dignity – and in my case, with a reasonably clear conscience.

2–4

Telephone Chatlines

Being a cross-dresser and being lonely didn't mix, and as such, I became addicted to telephone chatlines in the 1990s.

I just needed someone with whom I could talk freely, without fear. An anonymous confidante with whom I could share my burden without the risk of a backlash. Via the chatlines, I could talk to someone at the other end who didn't care a jot about what I did or didn't do. A characteristic of such phone lines was that they always attracted drunks and weirdos of every age, shape and form, so my foibles probably weren't the worst that the chatline operators had ever heard. But such chatlines were also very expensive. At a pound a minute, as some of them were back then, the phone bills soon mounted up. However, I was single and free, and if that was how I chose to spend my time and money – bearing my soul to a complete stranger at the other end of the line – then so be it.

The important thing was that the woman at the end of the line didn't know me, couldn't see me and, therefore, I was unlikely to face any retribution from them at any stage in the future. Having an actual female friend to talk to would have been the ideal: someone who could advise me about my choice of clothes or make-up, or how I styled my hair. It would have been great to go out on girlie shopping trips together whilst in male guise, where it would look like we were shopping for her but were actually shopping for me!

The problem with such friendships was that they could always break down. There could be a fallout and your greatest secret could be compromised in the heat of the moment. It would demand enormous trust in that person, even during the good times, to know that they weren't accidentally slipping up and informing others of your alternative lifestyle when your back was turned.

But even with the anonymity of chatlines and though I was calling from the privacy of my own home, there was still the fear of phoning one of the lines and finding that an operator recognised my voice – perhaps someone I had spoken to earlier that day or had drunk with in the pubs.

It sounds paranoid, I know, but that is my life as a cross-dresser – always fearing the worst. I phoned a chatline one night, and the girl who answered my call did sound amazingly like a girl who I worked with – our secretary. The last thing I needed, having confessed all my inner secrets, was for her to say…

'That's not you, is it, Paul?'

Imagine that! Thankfully, it never happened, but in the back of my mind, it was always a possibility that could never be ignored.

Whilst using chatlines, the majority of the operators would lend a sympathetic ear to my situation. In fairness, they were probably just humouring me.

"You're not hurting anyone," was the usual reply.

"Live and let live," was another response.

Many operators would tell me how their boyfriends wore women's gear. *Likely story*, I thought. It was just being said because the operator knew that was what I wanted to hear. Occasionally, though, I would be put in my place. I would get an operator that didn't hold back on speaking her mind.

"Hey, actually what you are doing is wrong," some would tell me.

This then led to some debate, and both of us would agree to disagree. But, more importantly, it was these types of responses that I felt reflected society's mood to cross-dressing more accurately than the positive comments that I had received.

"A man should be a man," one operator said to me.

"If I was a man, I wouldn't wear women's clothes," another remarked.

Like *she* would know.

"If you were my fella you would be down the road for doing that," another said.

The truth hurt, and I usually felt a little low having been told such things. The reality was, however, that these were the attitudes and opinions that drove me, and others like me, underground. These were the attitudes that would send me cowering behind locked doors with the curtains shut for fear of reprisals. Of those chatline operators who told me there wasn't a problem with what I was doing, I couldn't help but wonder what they would really think if it was their husband or boyfriend doing it? I feel sure it wouldn't have been all tea and sympathy then.

2–5

Burglary

Another fear I always had as a cross-dresser was being burgled. The wigs, the clothing and oversized shoes, as well as various books that I had collected on the subject matter, could all have given the game away if I did get broken into.

I have thought about what I would have done if I had come back from work one day to find *A Tranny Lives Here* emblazoned in large white letters across the front of my house. I imagined the scenario of burglars spraying it across my property in one final act of degradation. For this reason, coming back from holiday was always a real challenge. I would tense up as I got nearer my home. Would the world have found out about my secret in my absence? Were the last two weeks of holidaying bliss about to come to a sudden and disastrous end? I used to hold my breath as I anxiously approached my house.

Another associated fear was, having been burgled, the intruders escape via the front door, leaving it wide open. My neighbours, in being helpful, may have wondered why my door was open to the world and decided to investigate. Having entered my house to check that everything was OK, and being aware that I was a single guy, they would surely ask themselves why there were wigs, dresses and make-up in my bedroom.

Or, what if, upon realising I was a cross-dresser, the burglars had maliciously strewn my clothes and wigs all around my front garden? Would I be coming home to find my front lawn and bushes adorned with various items of femininity? How would I explain that?

A similar fear I have visualised in more recent times is having my car stolen. For, within the boot of my car, lies a sports bag containing my remaining feminine possessions. The days of having my own wardrobe dedicated to all things feminine have long since gone.

A single sports bag is what I have now been reduced to. If my car were stolen, there is every chance that the thieves would look inside the boot to ascertain whether there is anything worth taking. Seeing a bag would be an obvious draw as there may be cash or jewellery in it. Upon inspection, they would see the wigs, the clothes and the shoes. If I had carelessly left my name and address details on anything within the car, I may then be open to being blackmailed somewhere down the line.

And what happens in years to come when my young son grows up and wants to borrow my car? He may open the boot and inquisitively look into the bag. So, at some stage, I will no longer be able to store my items there for fear of discovery. But without that as a storage place, what would I do? I would be lost, cast adrift into a panic zone where I would no longer have instant, easy access to my alter ego. All that is to come, and I know I have to try and stay one step ahead and therefore store elsewhere.

True, these days, storage is big business and plenty of storage firms have sprung up in recent years that could offer a solution. However, many of these will require some form of identification upon contracting with them, including the provision of a home address. I am back to my dying scenario here, whereby I envisage my family receiving a letter a couple of weeks following my death, stating that I was overdue for rent on my storage. They would know nothing about it. Intrigued as to what I was storing, they would then make enquiries with the storage staff, explaining who they were and the fact that I had passed on. The bag would then be passed over to my family…and the rest does not bear thinking about.

Thankfully, the above scenarios of burglary and theft have, thus far, not occurred to me, but I did suffer indirectly as a result of my burglary fear…

2–6

Holidays

I used to keep a small A5 notebook that contained cross-dressing articles, news clippings and articles of interest. I also kept photographs of myself dressed en femme within, in what was basically a mini scrapbook.

Bearing in mind my fears regarding being burgled, I decided to take the book with me whilst on holiday on one occasion – just for safekeeping. But this created another problem in itself; I had the dilemma of what to do with it. Should I carry the book in my suitcase or take it through security with me? To put it in the suitcase ran the risk of the suitcase going missing, along with my secrets. Adding to that concern, I have, in the past, had my suitcase opened up by airport security staff once it had left my possession. Another concern was that I knew a guy who worked in the baggage department of our local airport. What if he were the one who opened it and recognised the pictures of me in drag?

Similarly, if I tried to take my book of clippings through airport security upon my person, I ran the risk of being searched. After all, I always set that X-ray bleeper off, even if I had removed every metallic object beforehand. A decision had to be made, and in the end, I decided that I would take the book through security with me. Again, I meticulously removed all metallic items before walking under the X-ray arch. My keys, my watch, my belt, neck chains, rings and money. But yet again, I set the damned alarm off.

A security guard approached me. He must have seen the horror in my eyes. He ordered me to remove any remaining items from my pockets and place them in a plastic tray. Along with my little scrapbook, the only thing I hadn't put into the tray initially was a couple of sandwiches. Stupidly, I hadn't taken into account that they were wrapped in tin foil. He searched me, ordering me to outstretch my arms. Satisfied there was nothing else on my person, he returned to the tray. He picked up my little book and slowly flicked through the pages.

There before him were my entire cross-dressing related newspaper clippings and magazine features, including advice on transvestism by agony aunts. The humiliation was unbearable. I didn't know what to do with myself, or where to look. The airport security man lifted his head from the book as he continued to turn the pages. He looked at me expressionless, yet in his eyes, I could see a lack of understanding – possibly even disgust. He then looked down again, continuing to flick through the pages, which now revealed photographs of me in drag. This occurrence lasted only seconds but seemed to go on for hours and hours. I was heartbroken – devastated.

That moment has to be one of the lowest points in my life. I felt so small, inferior and worthless. I had made a terrible mistake in taking the book with me, and it was all down to my fear of being burgled and being outed. My attempt to put a control measure in place had backfired gloriously. I try not to have regrets in my life and strive to take positives from every situation, but in such a scenario, this was difficult to do.

I suppose it could have been much worse. On this occasion, I was travelling alone; I could have been with my friends or family, which would have ended it all for me. I felt very belittled, degraded and extremely embarrassed as a result of what had happened. It wasn't the security guard's fault; he was doing his job. In fairness, with the nervy expression upon my face prior to being searched, he probably expected me to be in possession of a lot more than just a harmless little scrapbook. It was one of those extremely low moments that I experience from time to time. My confidence and ego had been knocked, and it was a very bad start to what should have been an enjoyable and hard-earned holiday. I was in somewhat of a depression following that incident and it spoilt the first evening of my holiday as a result.

Despite the humiliation of that incident, I still stepped things up majorly the following year when I went to the little Greek Island of Skiathos. It wasn't because I was stupid, daring or reckless. I was fully aware of what had happened the year before. It was because it was what I needed to do. I just had to do it. I had little or no control over my drive and compulsion and felt I couldn't survive for a week without physically being in touch with my feminine side.

Skiathos is the most wonderful and beautiful island, especially at dusk. I was again on my own, but on this occasion, I took some female clothing, make-up and a wig with me. Again, I stressed about my luggage going missing. As I was back living with my parents at the time, I had visions of it turning up at their address, opened or damaged with my items on view. If this were to occur when I was abroad, I would have no control over it. There would be no possibility of me intercepting it before my parents got to it.

But despite my concerns, the compulsion still got the better of me. The reality was, that it was far too hot to dress in Skiathos, anyway, as the heat was stifling. When I say 'dress', it was only going to be within the confines of my apartment. There was no way I was going to venture outside like that. At the time, I struggled with the idea of venturing out en femme in the UK, never mind on a tiny Greek Island with the different beliefs and customs of its locals. So the stress of taking that clothing and associated accessories with me was all for nothing in the end.

It was during that holiday, whilst I was in my mid-thirties, that I really started to take stock of my life. I no longer felt that time was on my side. I was by no means ancient, but I was no spring chicken, either. I hadn't settled with anyone previously, and what was more, there was no prospect of me settling down anytime soon. Friends of mine had met partners some years earlier and were in the early stages of bringing up families. Yet there was I, sitting in a Greek taverna on my own.

Whilst the lamb kleftiko was lovely, it would have been even better if I'd had some female company opposite me. I was very self-conscious about being alone, especially when dining out. That was my third consecutive holiday without the company of others. It was Hobson's choice, though: I either went on my own or I didn't go away at all. Being of a quiet nature, I struggled to mix with others and probably sent out standoffish vibes that deterred people from approaching me. I must have seemed aloof, stuck up and uninterested, but the reality was, I was just shy. I had become so used to not talking to people – especially about my secret – that I generally lost the art of conversation full stop. It was, therefore, a vicious circle. I feared at that particular time in my life I would end up being on my own. I was torn. I wanted a woman, but that would mean sacrificing or significantly curbing my dressing. The thought of it filled me with gut-wrenching anxiety and panic.

Before those days of holidaying alone, I used to travel abroad with a group of friends who lived in the North of England. On one occasion, I travelled up from London on the train in order to go on a fortnight's holiday with them. Upon arriving at my parents' house, I heard something that I really could have done without.

I think it was my mum who said, "We think we might go down to London whilst you're away and take in some of the sights. Do you mind if we use your house as a base?"

To say I went numb at the thought is an understatement. My mind flashed instantaneously to the wardrobe full of women's clothing, wigs and accessories that I had left behind. This was the last thing I expected or needed. My parents were, after all, living two hundred miles away. I therefore never envisaged such a situation arising – it just wasn't on my radar. My defence mechanisms had let me down due to my complacency. I was due to fly out with my friends the following evening and would be staying with my parents until then. What on earth was I to do? I was on the cusp of being discovered – and by my parents, of all people. I was in utter turmoil.

I was so dumbfounded by my parents' perfectly reasonable request that I could hardly string a reply together. I knew that I had no other alternative but to travel back to London the following day without them knowing. But this could have been fraught with problems. Firstly, it would mean that I would have to go missing for the whole day. I would need to come up with an excuse. But the main thing on my mind was what would happen if I ended up stranded in London? Supposing there was a problem on the railway line and I couldn't get back? All alternative means of transport were bound to be fully booked if such a situation arose. How would I explain myself? What would I be doing back down in London in any case – having not told them that I was going? I again had to formulate excuses in my mind, such as, *I thought I'd left a window open in my house.*

There I was again, with one lie leading to another. It was thirty-six hours before I went on holiday. I had travelled for nearly five hours to get to my parents' house, and I should have been relaxed and looking forward to two weeks in the sun. Instead, I was full of angst at what now lay ahead of me the following day. Not only was there the inconvenience of it all, but there was also the added expense of train travel. When I got to London, I would also need to pay for a taxi to and from the train station in order to save time on the underground. My heart sank, and I asked myself a question that I couldn't answer – *why am I burdened with such an affliction?* I was both desperate and unhappy.

The following day saw me once again back on the train to London. I had hoped to sneak out of the house without my parents seeing me but unfortunately, they asked where I was going. Thinking on the spot, I told them that I was going out to get some clothes for the holiday. The irony being that the clothes that I was getting certainly wouldn't be worn on that holiday! Travelling down, it suddenly dawned on me that having told my parents I was out getting clothes, I could no longer viably use the excuse of open windows in my London house. Subsequently, if I were to get stranded, I would now have no excuse at all. Plus, if I were unable to get back in time, I would be throwing away a holiday that cost an awful lot of money. This just added to the pressure of it all. Indeed, I felt ill with the resultant stress.

Having reached London, everything seemed to be conspiring against me. There was a massive queue at the station's taxi rank and having joined the end of that queue, I dithered in deciding what to do next. Should I wait where I was or should I take the underground? The latter would still leave me with a bus journey through the congested city streets. Whilst deliberating the situation, approximately a dozen other people joined the queue behind me. Psychologically, the taxi queue no longer seemed as bad and thereby appeared to be the best option – despite the cost that I was about to incur. After the longest quarter of an hour of my life, I finally got into a taxi and prayed for every traffic light to be on green.

Arriving back at my house twenty minutes or so later, I went straight up to my bedroom and opened the wardrobe door. There before me, hung my collection of feminine clothes. Usually, they offered me hope, light and pacification. But that particular day, it was like staring at a deadly poison. They were a noose around my neck, holding me back, creating me stress and forever threatening to expose me. It was those items that had once again made me lie, cheat and creep around – conning my parents. I was two hundred miles from where I should been and was living on a knife edge. And it was all because of those items that hung before me. How I despised them at that moment. But how I loved them, too.

There was no time to make a cup of tea or grab a quick bite to eat; I had to get straight down to business. As I looked at the array of clothing before me, I had a problem in what I was to do with it all – especially in such a limited turnaround time. My house was tiny and there was nowhere that could be construed as a safe hiding place. There was always the loft, but the hatch was tiny and there was no light inside it. It would be too time-consuming to even attempt to get the clothes up there. With time ticking away before I had to get my return train back up north, I had to think of something – and quick. I didn't possess a car in those days, so I couldn't even put the items in the boot for safekeeping. Whatever happened, there was no way I could let myself be caught in possession of those clothes.

Ten minutes later, I was doing the unthinkable. Having run out of feasible options – and my choice was limited from the start – I found myself frantically stuffing the clothes into my dustbin. I was full of regret. It was the most unnatural thing in the world for me to be doing. I had always collected feminine clothes, not disposed of them. Having done the dirty deed, I returned to the train station in yet another taxi. I hoped and prayed that there would be no delay ahead of me. I was on a tight timetable to ensure that I would be back in time for the early evening family meal.

For once, luck was on my side. After a day of four train journeys and two taxi rides, I was back with my parents, having been missing all day and without possessing any new clothes to back up the lie that I had told them earlier. Things had thankfully worked out and no challenging questions were asked. I was, after all, an adult, and if I were to go missing for the day, then so be it. But the stress of the situation was something I could have done without. A whole day was wasted just in order for me to cover my tracks and the toll that such stress takes cumulatively in the longer term remains to be seen.

Returning from my holiday a couple of weeks later, I stared at an empty wardrobe. I was heartbroken. That holiday had cost me more than I could ever have imagined.

On another occasion, again returning up north to holiday with friends, I left all my packing until the last minute. It was typical of how disorganised I was. It was a real rush trying to get everything ready, but I just about made it in time for the minibus to pick me up and take us all to the airport. I don't recall the resort that we went to that year, but, needless to say, it was in the Mediterranean, and it was hot. Upon arriving in our foreign land, we had a coach journey ahead of us.

As I sat back and took in the sights, I began to relax. I always worked hard and it was the thought of a good holiday that kept me going throughout the year. It was a lovely evening and dusk was taking a hold as we meandered through the dry, foreign countryside. The last residues of the day's sun were diluting rapidly into an ever darkening sky and the fragrances of olive groves and flowering shrubs wafted through the open windows of the coach as we passed them by. Occasionally, we would pass a tree full of insects that buzzed and chirped with enthusiasm, as though trying to impress us as we drove past. *This is great*, I thought, as I relaxed further into my seat. It was the beginning of two weeks of sun, fun and relaxation.

As I looked across at two female members of my group, sleeping after a long day travelling, I was suddenly wrenched from my relaxed state of mind with a sickening jolt. It hit me with such unbelievable force, for I realised I had made a terrible, terrible mistake. I suddenly remembered that I had left some items of make-up on show in my wardrobe, back at my parents' house. I was frozen to the spot, momentarily paralysed where I sat. It felt like that moment of absolute panic as you are about to fall backwards on a chair but manage to recover and regain your balance just in time.

The pain of the aftershock lingered for much longer, though. I was away for two weeks; what could I do? My parents were bound to go into the wardrobe at some point during that two-week period. The make-up was there because I had brought a small bag with me from London to take as hand luggage for the holiday. When putting items into the bag, I realised that I had left a lipstick, lip gloss, mascara and an eyeliner in one of the side pockets. I placed them in my wardrobe with every intention of either hiding them or, in the worst case, throwing them away. However, in my crazed rush to get packed and ready, I left them in there – in full view.

I had once again dropped my guard and left myself open to whatever was coming. I looked back at my two sleeping female friends, oblivious to the turmoil and angst I was now going through. They were both peaceful, recharging their batteries ahead of a fortnight of fun. Little did they know that, in a split second, my similarly relaxed state of mind had turned into one of absolute panic. I was envious – so envious that they didn't have to creep around like I did and were not burdened as I was. I realised that everyone had their own worries and I didn't wish stress upon anyone. But in the scheme of things, I also shouldn't have been so stressed about something as insignificant as a bit of make-up.

Those four small items tarnished that two-week holiday for me, turning my life upside down during that period. Four innocent items that weren't hurting anybody but were significantly affecting me. Whilst on holiday, my defence mechanism worked overtime in case I was asked who the make-up belonged to upon my return. I decided that I would blame it on a female friend called Jo. Whether my parents would believe me or not remained to be seen. Jo lived in Essex and my parents had never met her. I don't even recall mentioning her to them that much. They may, therefore, have believed she was some sort of imaginary friend, a figment of my imagination.

All the same, I had to come up with something. I decided to say that Jo and I had been away somewhere overnight and she had obviously left the make-up in my bag by mistake and I would return it when I saw her next. What else could I say? It was feasible, even if a little unlikely, because my parents knew that I wasn't exactly a huge hit with women. But as excuses went, it was the only one with any potential for credibility that would fit the situation I was in.

Upon my return home, two weeks later, nothing was mentioned with regard the make-up. As such, I will never know whether or not they saw it.

2–7

Television, Stress and Mini-Breakdowns

In the mid-nineties, a documentary was shown on television focusing on members of a support group for cross-dressers during their annual gathering in a northern hotel. For me, what I was watching was a scene of paradise. A large group of cross-dressers and their wives basically took over a hotel for the weekend. The freedom that they had compared to me, locked away alone in my tiny, darkened hideaway, was more than enviable. The documentary was immensely enjoyable and offered a great insight into the workings of such events from the comfort of my own living room. However, a few weeks later, over the Christmas period, I was with my wider family, enjoying the festivities and chatting about everything and anything as we so often did. Then the conversation suddenly switched to the documentary on the cross-dressers.

It started in a derogatory way and progressively worsened to guffaws of laughter about how daft and stupid the whole idea was of men dressing and looking like women. A roller coaster of emotions hit me as I sat there listening to their unwelcome banter. Anger and frustration were certainly two that were present. Their laughing, albeit unknowingly, at me and what I did, also hurt me. At that point, I really did feel alone in a crowded room. But the main effect was that I felt my neck, face and ears boil. I can't be sure, but considering how hot I felt, my skin must surely have gone bright red. I went so hot, I felt as though there were beads of sweat upon my forehead as my skin temperature continued to rapidly rise.

The laughter seemed to go on and on, lasting for an eternity. I so wished for the conversation to turn to another subject but it didn't. I willed someone to do something or say something that would distract everyone away from the topic of cross-dressing, but despite my wishes, my family continued to poke fun at cross-dressers and the whole scene that surrounded them. Whilst they continued to enjoy the hilarity of it all, I was suffering immensely. I felt exposed, as though everybody knew what I was about. It were as if I had been opened up and they could see my heart and soul. I knew that effectively I may as well have had the words 'cross-dresser' stamped through me like a stick of Blackpool Rock and felt that this was now on show to my whole family.

The more exposed I felt, the more I panicked – and the more I panicked, the hotter and more reddened my skin became. To this day, I feel sure I gave the game away by my inability to control my emotions and the subsequent reddening of my skin. I fear that they now suspect me, but I don't know and never will know for sure. I also fear that a similar thing could happen again. Since that incident, I have gone red with embarrassment in similar situations, but not quite on the same scale. I can control things a little more now I am older, but the fear of going through a situation like that again still remains with me. I am always conscious of that possibility in social situations, and it therefore ruins the potential enjoyment of those occasions for me.

Such fears, alongside the everyday stresses of cross-dressing, led to me hitting the bottle big time one evening, whilst within my London home. Dressed fully en femme, having consumed practically a full bottle of whisky, I slumped to my knees in front of a full-length mirror.

My shoulders jolted up and down as I cried silently but uncontrollably. Black streams of mascara began running down my rouged cheeks. I was a mess, both mentally and physically.

The constant carrying of my burden began to take its toll. I woke up facedown in the carpet the following day around lunchtime, unable to recall much from the night before. My head was sore and my throat extremely rough. I automatically had this fear of having done something stupid. Did I venture out into my cul-de-sac whilst en femme, singing 'There'll Always Be an England'? I honestly didn't know. I couldn't remember a thing. Did I phone someone, maybe a work colleague or family member, angrily and frustratedly confessing all? Again, I just didn't know. As nobody had been there with me, there was no one who could put my mind at rest. Nobody had kept me in check. The problem was that I could always be a bit irrational through drink, and for this reason, I hated losing control. But the one bit that did stand out was my mini-breakdown and that concerned me. How much stress was I under and what toll was it taking? The stress, plus downing a bottle of whisky, obviously wasn't good for me. My drinking had become excessive, I was smoking far too much and I was becoming somewhat reclusive. The truth was, I was all over the show – an absolute mess.

Many years later, I did happen to venture outside whilst dressed – in the city of Manchester. I was, however, fully aware of what I was doing and the risks that I was taking. It was all conducted in a controlled manner. Despite this, I still feared how society would react to me beforehand; what would have been the general reaction?

2–8

Public Reaction

Concerns as to how straight nighttime revellers can react to cross-dressers was demonstrated to me more recently. Whilst on a business trip in London, I saw a cross-dresser walking towards me in the busy West End. Curiosity was to get the better of me.

He was obvious as a cross-dresser and easily read. The problem was that he dressed too young for his age and wore a platinum-blonde wig. This alone made him stand out from the crowd, drawing unnecessary attention to himself. But that shouldn't have mattered. He should have been free to dress as he wanted, whether passable or not. He should have been free to walk down a city street dressed in such a way without fear or prejudice. In the real world, however, if I had been advising him, he would have presented himself far more subtly.

Purely out of interest, I followed this chap for a couple of minutes. I was intrigued to know what sort of reception he would receive in the cosmopolitan West End of London. In fairness, most people were too busy rushing around and wrapped up in their own business to even notice. Of those who did take note, many cast a sort of *is it, isn't it?* type of glance, but then returned to their own business without further interest. A young woman emerged from a bar, speaking on a mobile phone. She looked at the cross-dresser but continued to speak on her phone as if he weren't there. But then there is always one who has to spoil it all; one who can't live and let live, the one who feels the need to impose, intrude and inflict him or herself upon other people's lives.

In his attempt to show off to his two female companions, I noticed a black male in his late twenties begin heckling the cross-dresser. "By the way you're walking, mate, your knickers are too tight!" he shouted. The two females thought this was hilarious, which disappointed and angered me. They would have hated it if the tables were turned on them. If it were them being abused and harassed in such a manner by a strange man, they would have cried blue murder. Yet, because it was a male dressed in that way, they thought it was fine to laugh at their obnoxious friend's comments. This just encouraged him to continue the abuse further. After all, a man dressed like a woman is just some freak and ripe for such humiliation – right?

My disappointment in this incident was heightened because, as a black man, he should have understood what it was like to be on the receiving end of oppression; he should have understood the fight for rights and the feeling of being in a once-suppressed minority in a similar way that cross-dressers do today. But, despite this, he still felt the need to harass and bully someone who was merely walking in the street. Incidents like this just add to the fear of us venturing out.

2–9

Potential For Being Exposed

On another occasion, many years before, I recall returning back to London having spent some time up north. I stopped off on the way home for a couple of drinks in one of my old haunts. It was a lovely summer's evening, and rather than spend the whole of it on my own, cooped up in the house, I thought it would be a good idea to go and spend some time with some of my old drinking buddies. The regulars who were sitting around the bar were all older than me and I chatted happily to them, debated with them and even laughed with them – all of us suddenly experts in world affairs.

Despite me getting on well with the crowd, my radar picked up on a stream of quiet animosity emanating from a man sitting opposite me. He was older than me but younger than the group in general. He was probably in his mid-thirties, making him about ten years older than me. My eyes intermittently kept flicking in his direction to ascertain whether he was still glaring at me throughout the conversation. Sure enough, his eyes remained firmly fixed upon me. I noticed how he squinted each time he drew long and hard on his cigarette.

He remained quiet throughout the group discussion. I had seen him before and knew him from the pub. I didn't care for him much. There was a quiet friction between us each time we were in the same room. I don't know why. Whilst he wasn't my cup of tea, I had done him no harm, nor had he, particularly, harmed me. I just think he was one of those characters. He either liked you or he didn't. That being said, he hadn't curried favour with the rest, several months before, having stepped outside the pub for a fist fight with the landlord. Needless to say, he wasn't the most popular guy in the pub as a result – especially as the landlord was much older than him and wasn't in the best of health at the time.

A change in the pub's management saw him being allowed back in, following a period of being barred. So there he was again, sitting back where he always used to sit, as large as life. Without warning, the doors to the pub suddenly flew open and in breezed a much younger, fair-haired male, approximately eighteen years old. He walked straight over to the man sitting opposite me. I formed the impression that it was a father-and-son relationship. I didn't have to wait long to find out, as the older one slowly began staggering towards me, followed closely by the younger male.

"Have you got a problem?" he asked me in a projected voice. By his demeanour, he had clearly consumed several drinks.

As I was sitting on a bar stool at the time, I looked up at him, before looking away again, saying nothing.

"I said…have you got a problem?" he repeated, this time even louder.

I looked at him and simply replied, "No."

The bar had now fallen quiet. Everybody knew what this guy was like. Other men sitting alongside me looked straight ahead at the bar, doing their best not to gain eye contact with my aggressor. They quietly minded their own business in the hope he wouldn't start on them as well. These were guys who had been laughing and chatting with me only seconds earlier, but now, at this moment in time, they had disowned me. It was fair enough; I understood exactly what they were going through and didn't expect anybody to get involved on my behalf. They feared for their own safety and this wasn't their argument. It was mine. As far as they were concerned, it was down to me, and me alone, to sort it out.

"I'll head-butt you off that stool," continued the man.

The intimidation had now clearly escalated to direct threats of violence. Rather disturbingly, I noticed that he was shaking with anger as he said it. His eyes were wide. I was no doctor but he seemed somewhat unstable.

"Go on, Dad, do it," said the younger male. "Look at him. He's disrespecting you." So that confirmed my earlier observation regarding the father-and-son relationship.

The male continued, "Did you hear what I said? I'm going to head-butt you off that stool."

"Really?" came my sarcasm-tinged, automatic reply.

I wasn't trying to wind him up in any way because I was concerned about the situation. However, my response possibly wasn't the best, given the position I was in. I didn't really know what to say. I had just been threatened with violence and this wasn't a rational moment for anyone present. Strangely, my vision became physically tunnelled at the time, perhaps as some strange sort of defence mechanism. Momentarily, I was less aware of what was going on to either side of me. I was disappointed because, in a situation like that, such a defence mechanism was only likely to hinder me. It felt as though parts of my body were shutting down in readiness to take a blow. If anything, my systems should have been stepping up a couple of gears, so my lack of readiness to floor this guy was most concerning.

"I'll put a blade in you," he continued, as the threats once again stepped up to a heightened level. "And you know what? I won't do time in prison. I'll do time in a mental hospital. I've already been in there once."

His face was extremely close to the side of mine as he spoke. I could smell his alcohol-soaked breath as he brought his mouth to my ear. Droplets of his saliva landed on my cheek as he continued to spew out his venom.

"Really?" I again replied.

My repertoire of witty or defusing answers just seemed to be evading me that night. My heart was pounding. I knew this guy was not one for bluffing but I also knew him to be a bully. He had waited until it was two against one before he tried his luck with me. His son was becoming more and more agitated, goading his father into launching at me.

"Go on, Dad…do him. He's probably the one who grassed us up (informed) to the Old Bill (police) before."

I didn't have a clue what he was talking about, but what I did become aware of, despite my somewhat tunnelled vision, was that while his father was in my face, the son was pacing up and down behind me, paying particular attention to my travel bag, which I had brought back with me. Situated at the foot of my stool, it was as though he were building himself up to swipe it away from me. This only worsened my fear of the situation. I became even more stressed and anxious because I had female gear in there. If that bag was taken or I was knocked unconscious, then all my items could be thrown around the bar in a final act of humiliation. Silks and laces could rain down in an impromptu lingerie shower.

What happened next, though, was so out of the blue, I wouldn't have seen it coming in a million years. An older lady, in her seventies, bellowed gloriously across the bar, "Leave him alone."

It was unexpected – totally unexpected. Her voice projecting across the bar like that snapped everyone out of their terrified daze. To the aggressors, it knocked them off course and stemmed their flow of aggression and intimidation as they looked at her, frozen to the spot. To me, it blew away the misty tunnel in which my vision had been so severely restricted. Suddenly, I could see clearly to my sides again. Pearl was glamorous and feisty. She would have been a stunner in her day. She marched over to my aggressors and stood toe-to-toe with the older man, all five foot of her. She wagged her finger in his face as he looked down at her with utter disbelief. "You're nothing but a bully and a trouble maker, Jim Chapman. You're not welcome in here. Now leave him alone!" Chapman looked like a scorned schoolboy being reprimanded by his teacher.

To this day, I am so grateful to Pearl for sticking up for me because I admit that I was concerned, both about being hurt and for being outed as a cross-dresser by my two aggressors. But Pearl had more courage than the lot of us in there that night, and I remain eternally grateful for her intervention, even over twenty years on from that incident.

It all became a bit of a blur following that. My aggressors at some stage left the pub but I couldn't remember them doing so. It was as though shock had suddenly taken over and I couldn't settle. I had been humiliated and my hand shook as I picked up my glass to finish my drink. I feared that father and son may return to the pub with others or come back with a baseball bat or other weapon. I therefore didn't want to hang around. I just had to get out of there.

As I left, I saw the father and son outside the entrance door. I strode past them. Strangely, the father was doubled over, as though suffering breathing difficulties, possibly having an asthma attack. The son felt the need to have the last word in view of his father being incapacitated and came out with a string of expletives as I passed him. I was never to go in that pub again. On the tube train back home, my mind was all over the place with adrenaline still pumping ferociously around my body. The whole situation had been magnified greatly by me having those female items with me.

The truth was, I'd had to take something with me on my trip up north because I couldn't bear to be more than a few days without access to such things. It would just have felt like I was going through cold turkey if I had. I would have spent those few days in a state of anxiety. Whilst I may not have worn the female items whilst up north, it was a comfort to know I had them with me just in case. That is how sad and decrepit I had become. Having such items in my possession whilst under threat of attack had sent me into a never-before-experienced sense of panic. Having the compulsion to cross-dress made me question my worth as a male and my masculinity at the best of times. But on that particular occasion, to have allowed those two to humiliate me – in front of all those people – and for me to be so scared and shaken by them, made me feel less of a man than ever.

Most men probably aren't fighters. Many may think they are after a few drinks when the bravado takes over, but they are not. I hadn't been brought up to fight. The truth was, with my height and strength, I probably could have put both of them on their backsides if I'd really wanted to. But incidents such as that just made me more embittered and withdrawn. I have had a life of people letting me down and disrespecting me. The quiet, indirect disrespect and intolerance that society has shown over my lifetime, because of my dressing, has just added to me being more frustrated and bitter. I have always felt as though I am swimming against the tide – taking on the world. I had gone into that pub for no more than a quiet sociable drink and was merely minding my own business. However, the impact of that night left my emotions reeling for some considerable time after – years, if I'm being truly honest.

Psychologically, I have always tried to counterbalance the enhanced feminine feelings that I possess. Therefore, the rebellion, the masculine job and the cavorting in downmarket pubs in some of London's toughest back streets were all probably a result of me unconsciously testing my own worth as a man. The sad truth was, when the heat was turned up, I couldn't actually hack it. I may have tried to prove I was a tough guy, but that couldn't have been further from the truth. And boy did I feel inferior to every other person in the world as a result.

2–10

To Tell or Not to Tell…

A definite fear of any cross-dresser is the potential adverse reaction of telling a wife, partner or other loved one of the desire or compulsion to dress as you do. To tell or not to tell – that is the question. I spent years looking for love but admit to having been somewhat half-hearted about actually wanting to commit. Years of yearning to be with someone were equalised by feelings of not actually wanting to move in or settle down with them.

The restriction that such an arrangement would place on me would have been too great – life-changing even. It was catch-22: I wanted love and a close relationship, yet still needed freedom and space in order to dress as and when I pleased.

Rightly or wrongly, I did tell my future wife, Donna, about being a cross-dresser. Unfortunately, we were both drunk and in bed at two a.m. one morning, around fourteen months into our relationship. Never one to do things easily, that was the worst time and place that I could have done the deed. Not that there is necessarily a good time or place, but two in the morning when you're drunk? That was not wise. Needless to say, Donna cried. Then she cried some more. In fact, she cried herself to sleep that night. Revealing my biggest secret at that time and under those conditions gave us nowhere to go. There was no room for meaningful explanation or discussion to take place.

Alcohol is a depressant at the best of times, and Donna probably felt as though her world had collapsed upon her. It is difficult to be rational about anything having consumed drink.

Even when sober, cross-dressing can be an emotive, confusing and divisive subject area. So what chance did we have, having consumed drink? I don't even know what I expected to gain by telling Donna. It wasn't as though I wanted to dress in the house whilst she was there. Any remaining piece of 'macho' left in me, although already somewhat shredded, wouldn't have allowed that. Yet still, I felt the need to tell her.

After a week apart, she again contacted me. We spoke and Donna told me that whilst she didn't necessarily agree with what I was doing, she was prepared to continue with the relationship. I suppose the benefits of telling Donna are that when she married me, she knew exactly what and who she was marrying. Also, if she discovered a piece of clothing that wasn't hers in my car or in the house, she hopefully wouldn't be jumping to conclusions about me having had another woman in those places.

But for every positive, there is a negative. In telling Donna, it destroyed much of my male confidence within the relationship. As a cross-dressing husband, it is difficult to take oneself seriously as the hunter-gatherer, the protecting tower of strength that is still stereotypically expected in a partnership today, even within a supposedly equal society.

I could probably dedicate a whole book just to this particular topic. It goes without saying that the subject of disclosing your true self is a fearsome – and what should be unnecessary – burden that constantly weighs upon most closeted cross-dressers' shoulders.

The fears relating to my cross-dressing occur on a daily basis, which is quite a cross to bear. The potential for losing your family, your job, friends, pride, dignity and masculinity – not to mention your looks and teeth in the wrong company – are all realistic fears for any cross-dresser. In an advanced, free-thinking and supposedly tolerant twenty-first-century society such as ours, that is a sorry thing to have to admit. Attitudes are, perhaps, slowly beginning to change, and there is a little more understanding and,

I dare say, acceptance than there was over thirty years ago when I first started. However, society's prejudice, misunderstanding and fear of those who cross-dress is so deeply entrenched that the satisfactory acceptance of me and others like me will not be achieved in my lifetime. As a result, I will always be driven to hiding behind locked doors with curtains closed and suffering the stress and fear of being exposed and ridiculed in silence. And for what? My biggest crime to society and, indeed, the world is having a liking for certain cuts, textures and styles of fabric.

Now lock me up and throw away the key.

3.
VENTURING OUT

3–1

Craving Acceptance

As a shy and somewhat introverted type of guy, the thought of me stepping out onto the streets dressed en femme still seems unbelievable, even today. Yet, in my mid-thirties, this is something I felt strongly compelled to do. I think that there is something of an exhibitionist inside many cross-dressers, even if you are usually a shy, retiring wallflower in everyday life. After all, what is the point in going to all the time and effort of transforming into your alter ego if no one else is there to experience it with you? It is like an opera singer performing to an empty house. If you are anything like me, you want to be admired, adore being complimented and crave being accepted as a normal human being – even if you are going a little off-piste in the dress code at the time.

At thirty-five years of age, the need to go out dressed was eating away at me. I found that I was filled with anxiety, not so much at the thought of actually venturing out and exposing my biggest secret to the world, but because it was such a deep-rooted compulsion that required fulfilling. There was a hunger and a drive that was becoming insatiable within me. The longer I left it and put off the inevitable, the more anxious, depressed and irritable I became. Having decided that I needed to go out somewhere whilst dressed, it was evident that I had a certain amount of thinking to do. Specifically, where would I go and how would I go about doing it? Fortunately, I did know a little about the cross-dressing scene. I had already read a number of books and magazines on the subject. I had also been a member of a national cross-dressing group previously and received some invaluable newsletters and information from them. However, the one option that I knew would never be open to me would be walking down a busy high street on a Saturday afternoon. I had to concede that I would be pushing things too far in doing that. Society's misunderstanding of the topic at hand, and its resultant bigotry, would necessitate me going further underground in order to fulfil such a desire.

3–2

From Angela to Manchester

Living in northern England, as I did at the time, meant that Manchester was the main conurbation that could accommodate my chosen activity. Over two million people lived in and around the Manchester area, and it had that big-city, cosmopolitan feel. What's more, it had a great reputation for hosting transgender nightlife. This was a place where I could be myself and no one would bat an eyelid – or so I had been informed.

The realisation that I wanted – needed – to venture out en femme for the sake of my sanity, meant that I would now definitely have to go ahead with it. There could be no turning back once I had set my mind on it. To have built myself up, only to then lose confidence at the eleventh hour, would send me plummeting into a deep, dark, solitary depression. The itch that required scratching would still be present, only much stronger. Plus, it would just mean that I would have to build myself up once again to complete the task on another occasion. But right then, things were very different. I felt somewhat drawn, like a moth to a bright light. I was older, more decisive, and there was a renewed vigour and determination about me. That is not to say that the thought of me, standing at six foot three inches in height, and stepping out onto the mean streets of Manchester dressed in that way, didn't make me break into a cold sweat – because it did.

I did my homework before the big night. I went to a lady who provided a dressing service to cross-dressers. Angela was in her late forties and knew the Manchester scene well. She had, in fact, been actively involved with it some years back. We spent some time talking about what I wanted to achieve from my session with her, and I told her about my desire to 'take my show on the road'. Whilst at the dressing service, I received many valuable tips on the application of make-up and general deportment. As I sat being transformed by Angela, I looked around at the Aladdin's cave of feminine delights. Silks, pearls, laces and satins adorned the little dressing room that we sat within. An open wardrobe bulged with an assortment of fabrics of all shades and colours – needless to say, I was in my element. This was my world, and I could have spent hours, if not days, in there, indulging in the different styles that Angela had on offer. But such dressing services didn't come cheap. The clock was ticking away, and I had to be realistic. It therefore made sense for me to only dress in the clothing which I intended to wear on my night out.

For about half an hour that day, Angela made me walk up and down in her tiny hallway, with a determination that I am sure was indelibly etched upon my face. I embarked upon refining my feminine steps, balance and deportment in preparation for my big night out. Intermittently, Angela would observe and advise as necessary. To stride like a docker when out and about would attract unwanted attention. At my height, I was already disadvantaged, so I didn't want to draw even more attention by having a manly walk and gait. Things had to be right. I was always going to look exactly what I was – a man in a dress. However, the key was to look like a man in a dress who carried himself well. I needed to look as acceptable as I possibly could.

As I daintily trotted backwards and forwards along the hall, Angela would chirp in with her words of wisdom – "Don't swing your arms so much" – before disappearing again into the kitchen. I concentrated as best I could: *Don't swing…my…arms…so much.* I felt as though I were playing the drums – trying to do four or five things at once. I was so focused that at times, I became totally unaware of my surroundings.

Having spent a couple of hours with Angela, I began to remove the make-up and reverted back to my male identity. With my training over, I knew the next time I put on that particular dress would be for the main event. The dress rehearsal, no pun intended, was well and truly over. As I left, Angela advised me to keep practising and perfecting my demeanour when I returned to my flat.

With my dressing session over, the countdown to my ventures outside had well and truly begun. I booked a room at a hotel in Manchester city centre to ensure that I at least went on the night that I had planned. I didn't want to merely drift past the anticipated date with no action being taken. I knew that there was no way I would want to lose money by backing out, so paying a hotel deposit was certainly an added incentive for me to attend. Weeks turned into days, which soon turned into hours, and the date of my proposed adventure was eventually upon me. Before me was a test – a very big test. I wasn't leaping out of a plane; I wasn't attempting a bungee jump. I was merely going for a night out. But due to how I intended to dress on that particular night, it was a very big test to me all the same.

During the afternoon of my venture, I parked my vehicle in the suburbs of Manchester and got the tram into the city centre. It was as though I were in a trance whilst sitting there – as though being beckoned by a master.

I must do this, I must do this, I thought.

As it was the month of March, the nights were still getting dark fairly early. This was ideal for me because it was crucial that my outing occurred under cover of night. Darkness would be a major part of my disguise. As the tram meandered through the rapidly darkening Manchester estates, I clutched my overnight bag tightly. I saw another guy with a similar bag to mine.

I bet his bag contains sports gear, I thought. *I bet there is no dress, wig or make-up in there.*

At that point, I began to feel low. *What am I doing?* I asked myself.

I felt guilty, as though I was letting everyone down. My parents, my family, but above all else, I was letting myself down. I had never wanted for anything. I had been brought up well. I had been fed, watered, educated and comforted by the most loving of parents, and this was how I was repaying them. Sneaking around in a lifestyle of which they would never approve. They were old school, but more than that, they would have feared for my safety. All the same, I was still drawn – mesmerised by what I had to do – like an assassin focused on a mission.

There had, after all, been weeks of buildup to this night. As I had done previously, I attempted to comfort myself and justify my actions by believing that I would do it just once. I would get it out of my system, and there would be no need to do it again. I had always wanted to try most things in life at least once, and this would just be one of those occasions, something I would look back on in years to come.

After twenty minutes or so of battling with my conscience, I snapped out of my daze. The tram began to slow, and as I looked out of the window, I saw that the buildings were getting taller and the lights were getting brighter. We were approaching the city centre. This was the stage, upon which I would perform later that night. The butterflies within my stomach had started to flutter with an energy rarely experienced. To not go ahead with it, however, having gone that far, would have been an unmitigated disaster. Following a further minute or two of crawling, the tram came to a stop and it was time to make my way to my hotel. Excitement and anxiety continued to battle it out in the pit of my stomach.

3–3

Reconnaissance

The gay quarter of Manchester is based around the Canal Street area of the city centre. Here lies an array of small hotels and trendy wine bars and restaurants that are transgender friendly. Having booked in at the reception of my hotel, I made my way up to my room. Throwing the door open expectantly, I was soon to be disappointed with what I saw. The room was dingy and cramped. There was a single bed, a wardrobe and a small side table. Whilst a glass window was present, it was opaque, and from what I could make out, it was apparently facing the wall of another building. The shower room was tiny. The room's one redeeming feature was that it had a fantastic, brightly lit mirror situated above the side table. It felt as though it were a dressing room mirror from a theatre. I needed a good mirror and associated lighting as it would be there that I would transform before appearing upon my own stage – the streets of Manchester. Having dropped off my bags in my hotel room, I made my way outside, to get a better idea of the location. I surveyed every detail with precision, as though I were planning an armed robbery later that night.

The first thing that became obvious was that my hotel was located a little way outside the main area, possibly by a couple of hundred metres or so. That was a poor start for me. I had hoped that I'd be closer to the gay village and, ideally, within it. Whilst facially I could be classed as passable when made up – especially in a poor light – my height would always be the dead giveaway. This would always draw unwanted attention. A couple of hundred metres under certain circumstances is only a short distance, but bearing in mind my intentions, it may as well have been a couple of miles. I would have to walk through a small amount of 'straight land' before I reached the relative 'safety' of the village.

I plotted which way was the most direct to my destination. The shortest route would involve me walking for about twenty seconds along a busy, well-lit, main road. Then, by complete contrast, I would turn off the main road into darkened, isolated back streets. These were the types of streets I'd have thought twice about walking when in my male guise, never mind while cross-dressed. At that point, I recalled seeing a documentary only a couple of months earlier, in which gay men had recounted being attacked whilst leaving the Canal Street area. Those dark, quiet streets were prime territory in which this could happen. Anybody could have been lurking there.

However, before I knew it, I was in the gay quarter. It felt cosmopolitan, a touch continental, despite the cool March air. It was about six p.m. as I walked around. I tried to imagine what it would be like walking around there later, dressed in female attire. The butterflies again began to flutter. After walking for a few minutes within the gay quarter, I saw my intended destination – a small club that was situated above an exclusively gay bar. A female door supervisor stood outside the entrance to the lower gay bar. The club that I intended to attend that evening was a renowned meeting place for cross-dressers. It was a place that offered a safe haven to chat and mix with others of a similar ilk. My intention was to start the evening off in there, and then, if all went well, I would perhaps move on elsewhere.

First of all, I had to confirm that the club still existed. The last thing I wanted was to venture out en femme to find that the club was no longer run on that night or had changed locations. I asked the door supervisor for clarification and thankfully, she confirmed that the club was still there, situated on the first floor. I breathed a sigh of relief because, apart from the distance of the club from the hotel, all appeared to be going to plan. I was aware that hours were now turning rapidly to minutes, and it wouldn't be long before it was time for my alter ego to make an appearance. I therefore had to start psyching myself up and for that, I needed a drink…or maybe three.

In any case, I wanted to get accustomed to the gay bar scene in order to ready myself for later that evening. I wanted to see the layout of one of the prospective venues. I wanted to hear the noise and immerse myself in the atmosphere, whilst all the time looking out for potential escape routes and CCTV cameras that may record my every move. This, of course, was in the days before YouTube, but even so, I still had a thing about being caught on camera. I saw a large corner pub/hotel, which I recognised from my earlier magazine readings, and decided to give it a try. I was nervous about entering, though, in case I was seen by someone I knew. What would I, a straight man, be doing in a gay bar in Manchester on my own on a Wednesday night? Of course, it could be said that if they were in there, then they, too, would have some explaining to do. Well, not necessarily. More and more straight people were beginning to frequent the village, but admittedly, they would normally be in a group as opposed to being alone. A group of straight people could be in there for any reason, such as a birthday celebration or on a pub crawl. Being on my own would arouse suspicion. What could I say?

'This is a gay bar? You're kidding me! I didn't realise!'

Likely story, they would think.

This one probably wouldn't help my situation much either:

'No, no you have me completely wrong – I am not gay, I am merely in here because I will be dressing as a woman later…'

No. If I was caught in there, that was it. I would effectively be outed from that moment onwards.

Despite the anxiety of being caught, I gritted my teeth, hoped for the best and pushed open the entrance door. There were two bars within; one appeared to be larger and busier than the other.

There were a few seats – well couches, to be precise – as well as a few bar stools, but on the main, the venue appeared to be geared up for a night crowd. A large roller shutter cut off half the area; I guessed that the clubby part was located behind it.

There were approximately twenty people inside, mainly male. Some played pool, the rest hung around the main bar itself. Finding a space, I slotted in, ordered my drink and did my best to blend in. Subtly, I looked around at the array of faces in there. Thankfully, none of them were recognisable to me. Even though there weren't that many people within, the bar was still noisy – filled with excitable chattering and laughter. A jukebox played, which added to the overall atmosphere. One or two of the clientele appeared to have been propping the bar up all afternoon and were beginning to look a little ragged around the edges.

As I uneasily stood at the bar, I tried to imagine myself standing there later that evening, dressed en femme. How would I look? How would I feel? After all, this was to become reality within a very short period of time. With each opening swing of the entrance door, my insides went tight. Would I know the person or persons that were in the process of coming in, and what would happen if I did? Did I have an escape route?

Having consumed a couple of drinks, I flung open the swinging exit door and strode out into the cool, dark air of early evening Manchester. The door swiftly closed behind me; the cacophony of jukebox noise and excitable chatter and laughter was cut short, replaced by the low drone of Manchester's evening rush-hour traffic. As I made my way back to my hotel, I was content that my surveillance exercise was complete. I had savoured the atmosphere and established that all systems were go. I had established the layout of the area and the location of the bars that I had read about previously.

3–4

Metamorphosis

I returned to my hotel room, closing the door. The time had arrived. Looking into the mirror, I remembered that this was to be the ultimate test. If I could do this, I could do anything – anything at all. That having been said, there was another voice in my head, saying, *you can still pull out if you really want to.* But I knew that wasn't a realistic option. Certainly not at such a late stage. My eyes diverted to the digital clock by my bedside. I had around an hour to change.

I took out the array of make-up that I had accumulated over the years. All odds and sods, different brands, different qualities. Most, however, were at the cheaper end. Purchasing make-up from a shop was difficult for me. It is such a personal thing that ordinarily, a man wouldn't buy make-up for a loved one. I therefore felt that it would be too obvious for me to purchase from the counter of the local Boots the chemist. Jewellery, yes; that was a much safer option. At that particular time, online retailers were in their infancy, and as a result, I had to do my best with what I had. As I recall, Angela had also ordered a few items of make-up for me following my visit to her. She was certainly a handy contact to have.

Whilst I am a strong believer that a cross-dresser should be free to walk out in a dress whilst sporting a large beard if he wants to, I believe the main reason that we do it is to look more beautiful, more colourful and more pleasing to the eye. Therefore, if a job is worth doing, it is worth doing right. Time had to be taken getting the blank canvas spot on, in order to effectively build upon it. This process was always an exciting one for me: applying the colours to the 'canvas', blending them, adding to them. I have always loved colour and pretty things, be it a lovely sunset, a Christmas tree or an immaculately made-up face, especially around the eyes. I love seeing eyes brought to life with eyeliner. Part of the excitement is seeing the transformation into a totally different character, much like a butterfly emerging from its cocoon. But would I get the same satisfaction by transforming myself into a clown, or an old man, or by painting the cross of St. George on my face? The answer to that has to be no. So clearly, it wasn't just the stand-alone transformation process that made me do what I was doing. It was the transformation that made me look like a woman that was the driving force in my life.

After about an hour, my feminine persona really began to take shape. I had started with the eyes, applying eyeliner, and then encountering the obligatory struggle with mastering the top lid. Then came the eye shadow, blending in two shades of brown, with a touch of white. The mascara was next, enhancing my already long lashes further. They did need enhancing, though, because, in their natural state, they went very fair at the end. How disappointing is that? Then came the lips, and as I looked in the mirror, I found myself pulling the very same faces I'd seen numerous women pull when applying their make-up in the past. With a little lip gloss and precision-placed blusher, I was there. My face looked adequately feminine.

It was now time for the addition of a wig to cover my short dark hair. It had to be a good wig – an extremely good wig – which meant paying out good money. A cheap wig would not add anything to the character. Apart from height and stature, hair is the main difference in appearance between a man and a woman. Get a good wig that fits well and is styled correctly, and you're halfway there. The wig that I possessed at that particular time was a ginger shoulder-length bob, despite my natural dark colour.

I had always fancied trying out being a redhead, and if the truth be known, I didn't look too bad once it was applied. I had been inspired by photos of Toyah Willcox from the 1980s, noticing how her red hair complemented her darker eyebrows.

The transformation was immediate with the addition of the wig. I now looked completely different and instantly feminised. When made up, I looked quite good, so long as I resisted the temptation to get carried away in the process. It was easy to overdo it. Less is more and all that. There can be a fine line between looking like a great cross-dresser and an over-the-top drag queen. My main problem, though, was my height. If I was a foot in height less then I would have no problems. Sure, I was slim enough to carry off the look, but it would be others who would be judging me on that night.

All made up and dressed in a little black dress and black suede boots, I took one last look at myself in the mirror – one final check to ensure that all was in place – before I swung a handbag over my shoulder. Things weren't perfect, though. I had bought the dress via a newspaper offer some four years earlier, and it was now beginning to look slightly worn in places, but I loved it all the same. It was figure hugging and had a low plunging V-neck. Another problem that I had to be aware of was its propensity to slowly rise up my thighs either when lifting my arms or when sitting in a low, sinking armchair. Due to the chill in the evening air, I also wore a lightweight black nylon coat. Again, things weren't perfect with that. The arms were a little too short for my tall frame, but it was the best I could do. It is a problem with being tall and trans. You tend to grab the first thing that you like and hope that it fits. Ideally, it could be tried on first or you could seek help from a sales assistant. But being in the closet put paid to all that.

I pinned a pink breast cancer awareness bow to the lapel of my coat, and I was ready. I made my way to my room door and opened it slowly. Peeping out into the dismally lit corridor, I noticed the row of other room doors that were facing mine. As I looked to my right, the distance from my room to the stairs seemed ten times further than when I had strode along it earlier in my male guise.

The corridor was eerily quiet as I continued to peer out. *Now is as good as any other time to make my move*, I thought. This was a transgender-friendly, gay hotel, and yet I was frozen with fear – halfway in and halfway out of my bedroom door. *Please give me the strength. Please give me the courage*, I pleaded. But it was to no avail. I pulled back into the room and closed the door.

I leaned backwards, resting on the door itself, and looked to the ceiling in despair. This was my worst nightmare. Weeks of building myself up only to lose my nerve at the last minute. I gathered my thoughts as I continued to look to the ceiling and attempted to regain my composure. I felt so alone, with no support, no encouragement and not knowing what sort of reception I would get once I did manage to venture out.

Focusing on a dark strand of spider's web gently swaying in the corner of the room, I again began to build my strive and determination. I reopened my hotel room door and peered into the corridor. There was only one way for me to go, and that was to go forward. I just had to do it. To have retreated back into my room for the night would have left me at an all-time low. I edged my way out of the door and into the corridor.

3–5

Hello, World!

Closing the door behind me, I felt a great relief to have even got this far. I had now started to take my first steps away from the security of my hotel room. I felt as though I was walking in slow motion. The deportment lesson I had undertaken with Angela had been temporarily forgotten. I was on edge, looking and listening as I moved further and further away from my room. Like a ship leaving its docking area, the sense of space between me and the safety of 'land' became more and more apparent. The corridor remained quiet, save for the occasional sound of a television emanating from my neighbouring rooms.

I cautiously continued to the end of the corridor and came to a landing area. A large, rather grand staircase led down to the hallway and main lobby of the hotel, which was, thankfully, very quiet. There were no hordes of people milling around, like some hotels in which I had stayed in the past. The scenario was, so far, ideal. All was quiet. I just needed to get out of the entrance to the hotel. Standing at the very top of the staircase, my right foot hovered above the stair below it. I knew the lobby area was clear; that was not a problem. But there was a small bar area to the left of the lobby, just prior to reaching the hotel's main entrance. I wasn't sure whether I could hear a low chatter of voices coming from within there. If that were so, and if people were standing at the bar, then I would be on full view as I passed.

My foot still hovered, but all now seemed quiet. Perhaps no one was in the bar and I was mistaken? I was about to begin my first steps down the stairwell when I heard a sudden explosion of laughter from within the bar. Thankfully, I was not in sight so I knew the laughter wasn't aimed at me, but it was enough to knock my confidence once again. There now sounded as though there were three or four people in the bar area.

I retreated backwards from the top of the staircase and stood in the corridor, dithering. My mind was racing, and I couldn't focus rationally in order to formulate a plan B. All that I did know was that I couldn't loiter in the corridors of a hotel dressed the way I was for much longer. Standing there like a quaking wreck, it suddenly dawned on me. It was obvious. Why was I trying to do things the hard way? There was a separate, smaller stairwell that led directly to a door at the rear of the hotel. On my earlier surveillance mission, I had ascertained that this door led straight onto an alley at the hotel's rear. The problem was, there was no glass in that door. I therefore didn't know whether I would open it to find myself marching straight into a group of marauding passers-by.

Having tiptoed down the back stairway, concentrating intensely on not falling, I eventually came to the bottom plinth. There was no hallway – the stairs led straight to the rear door. I put my ear to the door, listening for any street noise, but heard no sound. My hand hovered around the handle. I tried to open the door, but I lost my nerve each time. I was dithering again. My exit was meant to have been cleanly executed, yet five minutes after I had left my room, I had still not ventured outside. I looked back up the stairs, viewing how much I had achieved at that point. It was then that I noticed I was in full view of a CCTV camera. Anyone watching my indecisive dithering in trying to open the door must have found the whole thing hilarious. It is difficult to describe to a non-cross-dresser just how I felt in that moment. Probably the closest analogy for most of us would be standing at the foot of that stairwell naked, knowing you had to walk at least two hundred metres with as few people seeing you as possible before you made it to a safer haven!

With a sharp intake of breath and a not-so-ladylike shove, I opened the door. A sudden burst of determination and energy drove me out into the night air. Closing the door behind me, I walked and walked and kept on walking. I was totally focused on moving forward at pace, but also as femininely as I could. I didn't look around, not once. For the first time in my life, I was outside, on the streets, dressed en femme. My breathing was heavy and irregular, my heart was pounding. It was the best buzz I had experienced since first putting the tights on many years earlier, but with much, much greater risk. The back alley was cold and dark, but the main thing was that it was deserted. It felt great to feel the breeze around my legs and hear the rasp of my nylons rubbing together as I continued onward.

I soon realised that I was at the point of no return. I had to use all my experience to keep my panic at bay. Being trapped outside whilst in women's clothes had been a recurring nightmare for me over the years, and yet there I was, in that situation for real. I was also concerned as I knew people who worked and/or lived in Manchester. What if they happened to be driving past at exactly the same time that I was walking past? Whilst I was the last person they would have been expecting to see around there, and I was heavily disguised, I still had concerns that my cover could be blown. This was the high-risk part of my journey. This is where I would stick out like a sore thumb. In my heels, I was walking at six foot six in height. Under the tall, bright lights of the main road, I was totally unmissable. Thankfully, the usually busy road was fairly quiet by the time I got to it; the home commute had long since subsided.

I should have got a taxi, I thought as I continued along on autopilot. There was fear, both of being discovered and of finding myself being humiliated, or even worse, assaulted. There was also elation, as this was both my dream come true and worst nightmare mixed into one. But above all else, importantly, this was me; it was what I was about. I was achieving everything that I had wanted to do for such a long time. I was finally being true to myself and anybody else that happened to see me at that time. Years of secrets, lies and hiding behind closed doors had been blown away. *Hello, world, this is the real Paul Jason!*

I turned off the main road and made my way into the dark back streets that I had surveyed earlier. A car drove towards me. My dark, shadowy body was now highlighted by the vehicle's headlights. My shadow elongated behind me. It was a taxi. *What should I do?* I pondered. This was the first potential encounter since I had left the hotel. I toyed with the idea of crossing the road and diving into a doorway, but thought better of it. I had to face the music sometime, and now was as good a time as any.

The taxi slowed to a crawl as it approached me. Clearly, I hadn't got away with it. Whilst I knew that I would stand out, I thought that taxi drivers around the village would have seen it all before, and that I may have been left alone. The Asian-looking driver tapped lightly on his cab's horn in a sort of acknowledging way. He then raised his open hand in a further act of acknowledgement, before driving past, regaining his original speed. Was this a good thing or a bad thing? Possibly the latter. Even though the streets were dark, and the driver should have been concentrating on his driving, I was still obvious for what I was – a man in a dress. A similar thing happened with another driver soon after. Did I have a neon arrow pointing at my head accompanied by the words 'honk the tranny'? I may as well have done. Mind you, being six foot three and wearing three-inch heels was never going to allow me to blend in anonymously.

The rest of my walk was through brighter, more populated streets. This worked both for and against me. I was now in a busier part of the town and was on full view to everyone. It didn't put me off, though, because I was now in the gay village. I felt much safer walking down the infamous Canal Street. I felt as though I was amongst my own whilst in the gay community – a somewhat suppressed minority back in those days. However, despite feeling safer, there was still a certain amount of angst within me. I was still strategically turning my head away when strolling past a bar or restaurant, for fear that there was someone sitting inside who would recognise me. I passed people, both men and women, waiting for the abuse to start, but it never did. It was a major relief. Just to be accepted by being left alone was something I yearned for, and now it was actually happening. I guess, for many, they had seen it all before. Also, for first-time visitors to the village on that night, it was perhaps the kind of image and experience that they expected, maybe even wanted to see, and therefore, they weren't going to react in a hostile way.

Finally, I reached my intended destination. The same female door supervisor whom I had made enquiries with earlier greeted me with a cheery smile, opening the door and allowing me entry. My next task was to walk through the lower gay bar area and then up some stairs. Whilst the actual lower bar was two or three deep with revellers, the bar room in itself was not too busy at all. The revellers laughed and talked amongst themselves as I passed them by. Again, I waited for insulting or abusive comments to be shouted, but there was nothing. Maybe I had built it into something that it wasn't? Maybe it wasn't all about me after all? People were merely getting on with their own lives.

As I reached the top of the stairs, I should have been gaining confidence. I had, after all, just walked the gritty streets of Manchester and through the throng of merriment in the gay bar situated below. But just as it was all going so well, I completely froze, incapacitated with fear. The enormity of what I was doing suddenly hit me, in that I was a long way from the safety of my hotel. A large modern unisex toilet was in front of me. I could also see the function room that I was aiming to get to, but I had temporarily lost my ability to move. Two women came breezing out of the toilet and brushed passed me. They didn't pay me a second's worth of attention. The hairs on the back of my neck stood to attention. It was a feeling I had experienced a few years earlier, as a seasonally employed postman, when I had suddenly found myself cornered in a garden by a growling, snarling dog.

But now I had to do something to snap out of this state of incapacitation, and do it quick.

I fumbled around in my handbag and grabbed my mobile telephone. In the absence of a cigarette, this was my new crutch. I took out the phone and made out that I was trying to phone someone. It may sound crass, but it bought me that extra couple of seconds to compose myself and prepare for what lay ahead. With the extra few seconds provided, I had once again managed to gain some composure. Focused, and looking straight ahead at my intended destination, I strode into the function room. I was so fixed on making it to the bar, I walked straight past a little payment desk. I was later approached in relation to my accidental misdemeanour, for which I was most apologetic; I clearly hadn't seen it. I offered to pay but was excused on that occasion.

The room was large and busy, but in all honesty, it was too brightly lit. I hated bright rooms anyway, preferring more atmospheric lighting. Being so bright, it made me a little self-conscious about any flaws there may have been in my make-up. However, once inside the function room, I rapidly began to relax. It was the most relaxed I had been all day. The buildup and anticipation throughout had been somewhat draining, but for that moment, I was safe and felt secure.

Through the windows of the function room, I could see the tall office blocks of the city centre. It was surreal to think that only a couple of minutes earlier, I had walked the streets over which those offices towered. I needed ten minutes or so to reflect on my achievement, ten minutes within which I could gather my thoughts and take in my surroundings. Standing at the bar, I noticed a beautiful young barmaid. She was blonde, slim and gorgeous, and I later found out that she was, in fact, a he. I had entered that room quite pleased with my appearance, but compared to him, I was several leagues below.

3–6

Making Allies

The strange thing is how my behaviour would change when dressed en femme. Instead of ordering pints of lager, I would order half pints or glasses of wine. Whether it was a half pint or not, I certainly needed that first drink to soothe my shattered nerves. The bar was busy, and the beautiful one was the only one serving. After a couple of minutes, I had been served. I surveyed the room as I sipped from my glass. There was a whole spectrum of people in there. There were tall ones, small ones, larger ones and slimmer ones. Some were young, some were older, one or two were stunning, others had at least made the effort to enter into the spirit of things. One guy stood, as he was, in a black evening dress. He had no wig or make-up to enhance his image. It was just him, stood there for all to see. This to me was true freedom and equality. Here was a guy without pretence, without having to hide behind an alternative image. It was just him being himself in a dress.

As the minutes passed, I found myself grabbing quick bits of polite conversation with my peers as they filtered to and from the bar. Many seemed to know each other already, as though they were regulars at the weekly meeting. After half an hour or so, I was joined by Mary. Mary was attempting to get a drink, and we made small talk as he waited. Mary was a truck driver from down south who attended the meeting as often as he could. He was a little rough in his demeanour and told it as he saw it. No airs or graces. He was basically a rough diamond dressed in women's clothing.

Absolutely amazing, I thought. What drives a clearly masculine man to possess such desires that would make him dress in this way? It just goes to show that the old adage of judging books by their covers is as true today as it had ever been.

"Can I get you a drink?" he bellowed coarsely.

"That is very kind of you. Half a lager, please," I squeaked.

"Have a pint – it'll last you twice as long." He smirked.

So there we were, two regular guys, enjoying a pint but conscious that we may be smudging our lipstick as we did so. I thought that this was both extremely bizarre and amusing – *surreal*, even. At one point, I couldn't stop smiling at the hilarity of it all. What the bloody hell were we doing? It was totally crazy. I'm therefore not surprised that others outside the scene think the whole subject is both strange and amusing, too. If I don't understand it and can't work it out, despite years of thought on the matter, how can I expect others to understand?

You will notice that I refer to cross-dressers as either he or him. That is because they are, in the main, men after all. It is commonplace within the scene, however, for them to refer to each other as she or her. I disagree, perhaps controversially, with this side of things, because it just makes the scene all the more comical and weird – schizophrenic even. Having bored Mary with my not-so-popular views, I noticed that he was in need of a top-up.

"Another drink?" I asked, already turning to the bar in readiness. My confidence levels had now been boosted. I had been accepted by the group in general and was enjoying the evening. I didn't mix well as a rule. Yet here I was, doing what I was doing, going completely against the grain and being accepted all the same. Within half an hour, I was chatting and mixing – something I would usually have struggled to do, even after several weeks of propping up a bar in a straight pub. It was a little strange, because although I was being my true self, it wasn't me standing there, either. A different image changed my personality slightly – in a positive way. It goes without saying that the alcohol was an obvious help.

Mary and I continued to enjoy our drink, having a laugh, talking about football, women and the best deals on clip-on earrings.

"I don't need clip-ons," I announced proudly. "Both my ears are pierced anyway."

"How do you get away with that?" enquired Mary.

"Being a singleton," I replied. "There are no questions asked."

As the evening rolled on, Mary suggested that we move on elsewhere. At that point, I began to feel a little anxious again. It would mean leaving the relative comfort zone of the club I was in, and I hadn't had a chance to psych myself up. But I was no longer on my own, and I'd had enough drink to help control my anxiety. Surely things had to be easier this time? Thankfully, they were. It was always my intention to go elsewhere anyway, it just took me a little by surprise that it was to happen so soon.

We ended up going back to the pub where I had been earlier on that evening. It was about a minute's walk away. Funnily enough, I never wanted that minute's walk to end. Everything seemed so natural and in place. Being with a fellow cross-dresser was one thing, but being out in the big wide world was another. I liked being amongst the straight community while dressed, and with Mary by my side, the fear of what others would say or do lessened considerably. As I approached the pub, I noticed a bouncer on the door. He was smiling, courteous and welcoming, opening the door for us in a very chivalrous manner. I wouldn't have received such treatment as a male and I therefore felt a little bit special as I entered.

As the door swung open, the bar was much busier and louder than it had been before. Entering from the cooler outside air only exaggerated the body heat of the crowd within. A DJ played music at its maximum volume and shouted and hollered at the revellers who swayed and swivelled enthusiastically. The bar area was three or four deep, and I suddenly realised that, unfortunately, it was my turn to get the next round of drinks. As I stood awaiting my turn to be served, I felt very vulnerable. I had left the comfort and security of an all-transgender venue and was now in a gay bar. As a cross-dresser, I was in the minority and stood out like a sore thumb. It was a generally mixed crowd within there and included some real women. I believed them mainly to be straight but liking the vibrant gay bar atmosphere. The vast majority, though, were male. I got some inquisitive looks from the punters I was standing amongst but for the main part was left to my own devices.

This is going to take at least ten minutes, I mused, as I waited patiently. I was totally uncomfortable with the situation.

But just as all was going well, I was suddenly and rudely awoken from my thoughts. Some idiot grabbed my rear with force using both hands. With the ensuing shock, I practically launched into space. Looking behind with disdain, I saw a young shaven-headed male with his friend, grinning from ear to ear. Although I had just basically been indecently assaulted, I thought it best to ignore him. I suppose that was one of the perils of doing what I was doing. It was something that I would, unfortunately, have to accept. But I certainly wasn't happy with such an intrusion. I didn't treat people like that, and I didn't expect others to inflict it upon me. The fact I was a man in a dress wasn't an invitation for people to do as they pleased. Thankfully, he soon moved away, no doubt to pester some other poor soul.

That little episode ate away at me. I despised the audacity of that guy. It sounds clichéd, but to say I felt like I was treated like a piece of meat rang very true. Yes, I was a man dressed like a woman, but I didn't deserve that. I wasn't there to be abused or assaulted, and my confidence had been severely knocked. I eventually returned to Mary with our drinks. I didn't tell him what had happened, not wanting to create a fuss, but the incident left me in a subdued mood.

I stared across the crowded dance floor. The DJ was going down very well with the crowd, engaging with them by requesting votes for the next record that they wanted playing. After a short while, my mood began to soften again. I was glad that I was snapping out of it because being depressed whilst in public, en femme, was not a good place to be.

Mary and I were soon joined by another cross-dresser called Sarah. Sarah came out of nowhere to join us. He was younger than us and looked great, apart from one thing – a blue beard still being visible beneath his foundation. Like me, it was Sarah's first time out, and he was visibly nervous and inexperienced. I must admit, however, that I thought he was far braver than me, having entered a mixed venue on his own.

Sarah, Mary and I got on very well. I had met two people with the same interest as me. One of them was in the same boat as me, experiencing the same roller coaster of emotions on their maiden public outing whilst dressed en femme. As we stood chatting and people watching, we were getting the odd bit of attention ourselves. Some was welcomed, some less so. This was the case when we were joined by a small man, in his fifties. To be honest, he looked semi-vagrant. Whilst he was OK to hang around with if you were in a group, we could have done without him being with us for too long. He introduced himself to us as John, and it was evident that he was a bit of a tranny fancier. Thankfully, it was Mary who was on the receiving end of most of his attention. At one point, I overheard him say to Mary, "You have nice legs, can I run my hand along your stockings?" Mary replied that he would prefer it if he didn't. I thought this to be quite amusing and was certainly glad it wasn't me receiving such attention!

Scanning the dance floor, I noticed that we also appeared to be getting the attention of three women. With my usual self-doubt, I looked behind me, but there was no one else there. Now this I loved. I so wanted to be part of a girly night out. But bearing in mind how useless I was with women in nightclub scenarios generally, it was unlikely to be me that made the first move. The looks that we were receiving were certainly looks of interest, not perhaps a fanciable interest – but an interest in what we were doing and what we were about. Two of the women brought their heads together as one said something into the other's ear. The one receiving the comment automatically looked in our direction again. I just about overheard her say, "Which one, the red-haired one?" Well, that was me, all right. Mary was brunette and curly, and Sarah was dark and straight. The problem being that I didn't get to hear the first part of the conversation. It could have been 'Gosh, that one is ugly!' I do hope, however, that it was along more flattering lines than that. One can dream. Needless to say, as expected, it all came to nothing. They didn't approach us, and we didn't approach them. Their interest did continue for some time after, though; however, it has to be said that when they passed us later, it was obvious that they'd had more than a couple of drinks because one of them struggled to walk in a straight line.

The night rolled on and, having needed a comfort break for the last half hour or so, I could hold on no longer. I badly needed the loo, but what did I do in a situation like this? I had read that it was the etiquette in these places for cross-dressers to use the ladies' toilet. However, I felt the need to confirm this with Mary first. Neither was a good option. I certainly didn't want to go to the gents' dressed like this. Similarly, I was uncomfortable with the thought of using the ladies'. I had visions of me causing an uproar, sending women into a panic with my unwanted intrusion. Obviously, the last thing I wanted was to attract such attention and be ungraciously slung out of the place. But I had to do something, and do it before it was too late.

The ladies' it was, then – decision made.

3–7

Logistics

I entered the ladies' toilet somewhat tentatively, pushing the door open slowly. My face was surely grimacing, awaiting the screams and the sensation of half a dozen pairs of hands pushing me back out. As the door opened further, my hopes that the ladies' loos may be empty were dashed. I could hear chatter; I could hear laughter. There was excitement in the air. I joined the obligatory queue waiting to use the cubicles. I was sheepish in my actions, expecting the worst. However, it was amazing how matter-of-fact the other girls were at having me in their toilet. There were no screams, no angry responses, just girly-type chat and witty quips. It was just another night for them. They treated me in the main as though I were one of them.

"Crikey, how tall are you?" one girl asked.

As I outstretched my right leg, I said, "In these heels, I'm about five foot eighteen inches." I could see her desperately trying to work my answer out.

Standing there with the other girls was great. I had entered a different world – a world in which they would escape to gossip about others or reapply their make-up. But the best thing for me was their acceptance and tolerance of me as a person, as well as for allowing the use of their personal space. For that, I was most grateful.

Having got the dreaded toilet scenario out of the way, it was again time for us to think about moving on to another venue. John had drifted off somewhere amongst the crowds around the dance floor, and this was our chance to escape from him once and for all. We seized the moment, and Sarah, Mary and I made for the exit. Our quick escape from John's clutches brought a smile to my face. By the door through which I had walked into the cool air earlier that evening, I stopped, paused, and took one last look towards the crowded dance floor. I had enjoyed the experience of that dance bar immensely. It was a touch of reality, in that there was a mixed crowd in there. Apart from the incident at the bar, I would surely treasure those memories forever.

Walking towards another bar, apprehension again took over as I saw a group of men walking towards us. There were five of them, and they were somewhat rowdy in their behaviour, laughing and shouting as they strolled towards us. I formed the opinion that they'd had a drink or two. But in unison, they fell quiet – each and every one of them. They had spotted us. They continued to walk towards us in silence, as we did with them. It felt as though I was on a film set, and we were in the process of filming a bizarre type of gun duel. There was no opportunity to turn back or dive into the shadows. They had seen us, simple as that. There was only one option and that was to keep walking towards the men.

What's Mary thinking? I wondered. *Surely he's been in this position before?*

As he was the most experienced, I decided to follow his example and also stayed quiet. There was no point in trying to make small talk in a situation such as this. We all needed to concentrate, but more than that, we needed to put over an air of not caring, of being strong, despite how we looked. The silence between them and us continued until we were right upon each other, practically eyeball to eyeball. The reality was, however, that in an attempt to avoid potential trouble, I avoided eye contact at all costs.

"Good evening, gentlemen," came a sarcastic quip from the group's main mouthpiece, in a 'you don't look good enough to fool me' kind of way. He was being a smartarse, of course. All bravado in front of his mates.

"Good evening," we replied, in our deepest voices, psychologically suggesting that we may look as we do, but we would still put up a fight if need be. Thankfully, it all came to no more than that. The mouthpiece was happy that he had stamped his mark on the situation. Looking on the bright side, it was better than him stamping his mark on my face.

Having reached what was to be our final venue of the night, I noticed that the downstairs bar to the club was trendier and more lounge-like than the previous one we had been in. Neon lights gave it an overall blue aura. The atmosphere was more laid back than before. As the latest transgender trio to enter the bar, we were again getting attention but it was more subtle than earlier. There were occasional glances checking us out but those glances would soon melt away again. There was complete acceptance in there. I again felt relaxed in what appeared to be a mixed crowd. Above us was a nightclub, and the thud of the raving bass beat could be heard from where we stood below.

Mary, Sarah and I chatted like we had known each other for years. I had found two people with whom I shared a common interest and indeed secret. Keeping all this hidden from society had been a strain for me over the years. I had become very much withdrawn and closeted, believing that I was out of line with everyone else. It was a lonely feeling. Yet here I was, enveloped in clinging fabrics, being accepted by a mixed gay and straight crowd whilst in the company of two like-minded individuals. Suddenly, I was no longer lonely, withdrawn or isolated. I was in seventh heaven.

Clunk went Mary's clip-on diamanté earring as it fell to the darkened floor.

"Did you see where it went?" Mary enquired.

All three of us scanned the floor. It seemed to be to no avail, but then something glittery caught my eye – and there it was.

"Found it," I proclaimed proudly.

Without a second thought, I began bending down to pick up the fallen piece of ear decoration. Needless to say, the counter-effect to that reaction was that the hemline of my dress began to rise up my thighs at an unforgiving speed. I slammed on the brakes. Another inch or two would have exposed my derrière to the rest of the world, and I didn't want to inflict that upon anybody. To say I was sorry that I had started the retrieval of Mary's earring was an understatement. This was something that had to be approached with precision. I passed Sarah my drink as I anticipated how I would solve my little conundrum. As I gently pulled down the hem of my dress with one hand, I performed a kind of curtsey in order to pick up the earring.

I must get a better-fitting dress, I thought as I awkwardly began to rise again. *That could have been embarrassing.*

Mary wasn't one to hang around in one spot for any length of time – that much I had ascertained about him – and we soon moved upstairs to the main nightclub part of the venue. It was tiny and much darker than the downstairs bar. It had a very small dance floor and a small bar. A noise that could loosely be called music blared from the DJ's speakers. Feeling a bit tipsy, I switched to soft drinks. It was a sobering thought that the main part of the night was now behind me, and I would soon have to embark upon my enduring walk back to the hotel. The company I was currently enjoying would not be with me in half an hour's time.

I noticed that the nightclub was more hardcore than the last dance bar we had been in. A number of men were stripped to the waist as they gyrated and smooched with others on the dance floor. This was all a bit too 'scene' for me. The club was OK, but it lacked the camp, girly, party-type atmosphere of the last bar that we had been in – and there were fewer real women present, which was a major let-down for me.

Then, out of the darkness, emerged a familiar face – it was John. He had caught us, bang to rights. John was OK, but as I was now starting to get anxious again, I didn't really want to be engaging in small talk. I finished my drink. John offered me another, to which I thanked him but politely turned down the offer. It was now very late, and I had to think about my exit strategy. The best thing would be to get a taxi, but I had visions of having to stand outside a taxi office, enduring the wrath of drunken revellers. The comfort and security of the last few hours in the company of Mary and Sarah would be sorely missed. There was definitely some merit in the saying 'safety in numbers'.

The crowds within the club were now diminishing significantly, and it was time to make my move, whether I liked it or not. I bade farewell to Mary and Sarah, who were lingering until the bitter end. They were staying in hotels at the other side of the village to mine, so there was no point in remaining any longer with them. Before I left, I swapped mobile numbers with Sarah. I would have swapped with Mary, too, but he was a bit more flighty. It struck me that he would probably be with somebody else the following week, and we would be forgotten about. I had no intention of venturing out again under these circumstances, but I also hated goodbyes. It was nice to know that I could hook up with Sarah again, if the desire grabbed me. I began to make my way downstairs when I heard John say that he would come with me.

"No, don't worry, I'll be OK," I said.

After all, I didn't want him distracting me from my thought process in tackling the short walk back to the hotel.

"It's no problem. I'm leaving now, anyway," he replied.

Part of me was exasperated that he wouldn't take no for an answer, but a larger part of me was glad that at least I wasn't leaving the club on my own. I did feel guilty, as I was glad to get rid of him earlier, yet now, in many ways, I could perhaps be viewed as just using him. But John seemed happy enough with the arrangement.

"I'll walk you back to your hotel," he said.

"Honestly, John, you don't have to," I said.

"No it's fine, not a problem," he insisted.

Walking back, John talked about everything and anything, whereas I just wanted to concentrate on what I was doing. As we made our way past a taxi office, there was a drunken male and female sitting on the steps outside, smoking cigarettes. I expected abuse from this encounter, especially as her drunken slur could be heard all over town. *Here we go again*, I thought. Another potential conflict. The couple's eyes obviously couldn't focus clearly upon anything of a slight distance. We were practically walking level with them before I heard the woman's drunken call.

"Oi. Daddy long legs!"

Was that it? Was that the best she could do? Here I was, walking the streets of Manchester en femme in the early hours of the morning, and that was as bad as it got – Daddy Long Legs! In truth, I was relieved. Whilst I would have preferred no comment at all, it could have been much worse. I was glad to come away unscathed. John continued talking as though nothing had happened; as for me, I breathed a sigh of relief at having survived another potentially difficult situation. Walking for another few minutes, we reached the front entrance of my hotel. I thanked John for accompanying me back, wished him well and told him to take care of himself.

As he walked away, he turned and shouted, "You know what? You are gorgeous. Do you know that? You are absolutely gorgeous!"

It made my night. It was the icing of all icings on the cake. As I watched John walk into the distance, I took one last look around at my stage. It had been a decent performance. The bustling city centre streets through which I had ventured earlier were now deserted, save for the odd passing taxi. Pushing at the front door to the hotel, I was stopped in my tracks. It was locked. I didn't panic, as I saw a night porter walking towards me. He greeted me without a look of shock. He had clearly seen it all before. I was past caring, in any case. The alcohol consumed throughout the evening had seen to that. The hotel foyer was now darkened and quiet. I walked up the large stairway upon which I had hovered with anxiety earlier in the evening. It was astonishing to comprehend the difficulty I had experienced.

Turning into the dimly lit corridor, I had made it. I had achieved my goal. Entering my room, I was back where it had all started. I removed my boots and collapsed on my bed, shattered. I stared at the ceiling, to which I had earlier looked for inspiration. With John's departing words still ringing in my ears, I couldn't help but smile. It had been a fine night – a thoroughly enjoyable and extraordinary night. There had been bizarre moments, and there had been anxious moments, but it had been brilliant all the same. My mind was overly active, though it was definitely time to sleep. But as tired as I was, that night's sleep was bound to be somewhat disturbed.

Looking into the mirror, I removed my wig and jewellery. I continued to reflect on the events that had occurred throughout the evening. Cleansing my face of all make-up, I felt refreshed once again. I loved applying it, but it was always nice to remove it as well. The blank canvas had once again returned. Drag had turned back to drab. Turning the room lights off and settling into bed, the quiet of the night was replaced with a ringing in my ears; the noise from the nightclub's speakers had taken its toll. I woke the following morning on a high from the events of the night before. I had completed my challenge of going out dressed en femme and was very much content with myself and generally at ease. I felt clear-minded and unburdened.

3–8

Surveillance

As it happens, I did return to the Manchester scene whilst dressed on a further two occasions. However, I was never to meet up with Mary or Sarah again. A year or so following my first outing, I was standing in a pub in male guise, when I saw something that would curtail any potential for future outings whilst dressed en femme. I couldn't believe what I was seeing. A guy standing near me showed me his latest purchase – a mobile phone. But more than that, it had a camera incorporated into it. He had taken a picture of me without me even knowing. This was a first. Up until that point, phones didn't have cameras. If anyone took a photo of me previously, I would have known about it. They would have had an actual camera in their hands, pointing it in my direction. In low light, there would have been a very revealing flash. But this mobile phone had been so covert, I was completely oblivious to it having been used. My mind raced with 'what ifs'. I clearly couldn't take the chance of every Tom, Dick or Harry taking a sneaky picture of me whilst en femme in future. The reality was that it was only a matter of time before everybody would possess such a camera phone.

As such, the progression of mobile phone technology brought my newfound passion for venturing out en femme to an abrupt and very regrettable end.

4.
TRYING TO MAKE
SENSE OF IT ALL

4–1

Cross-Dresser, Transvestite or...?

I don't like being labelled. I am a person, not a thing. However, I have still used the two most common labelling terminologies within my writing – those being 'transvestite' and 'cross-dresser'. This is not necessarily because I agree with such references, but for greater ease of understanding. They are generally recognised descriptions for what I do and the life I happen to lead. 'Transgender' or 'trans' are umbrella terms which are probably less derogatory on a personal level, because I can't deny having a foot in both gender camps – even if I don't want to transition from being male.

The term 'transvestite' sounds so seedy and distant. It's like carrying an awful disease for which one requires segregating from the rest. It conjures up visions of the antisocial or the sexually deviant. And whilst there are undoubtedly a number of men that use female clothing to achieve their ultimate kinky aim, I believe those to be fetishists – hairy panty wearers, as they are sometimes known – a completely separate entity indeed. Female clothing just happens to be a turn-on for them, just as leather or bondage may be for others. I don't believe them to be transvestites or cross-dressers in the true sense of the word. The whole compulsion to take on a feminine image is much deeper than brief moments of sexual or masturbatory gratification.

The term 'cross-dresser' was unknown to me early on in my dressing experiences, hence why there is some reference to 'transvestite' in my recall of my earlier years. After all, that was the only common reference to those who dressed in clothing of the opposite sex back then. But of all the labels that I could actually be given, such as 'nice guy', 'family man' or 'loving father', the one that most wants to stick on me is one of the two listed above. Even if I only cross-dressed once a year, or was caught in the act just once in my lifetime, that is the label I would be given from thereon in. In contrast, if I played golf but once in my life, the last thing society would grace me with is the prestige of being called a 'golfer'.

Society needs to compartmentalise and allocate into different sectors. By labelling me in such a way, it highlights me as being different from the rest. It demonstrates that I am part of a minority group, places me to one side as one to watch. After all, society is still unsure and wary about the likes of me. Doing what I do is merely an extension of my personality – no more than that. Yet, the nastier side of society will pin even worse labels upon me. I may be labelled as a 'pervert', a 'weirdo' or 'queer'. The press label what I do as 'kinky' or 'gender-bending', in their usual sensationalist way. As such, the true worth of me – the caring, genuine, humorous side of me – is unlikely to be recognised as the main side of my character. I am moralistic, law abiding and well mannered – qualities that can be so lacking in today's society, even by people who don't have to suffer such defamatory labelling – i.e. those considered as being 'normal'.

I prefer giving, as opposed to taking, and I have time for people when others don't. I recycle to the point of compulsion because I care about the Earth and the effect we have upon it on a daily basis. I believe in creating a chance for future generations, so that they may live in a cleaner, less wasteful world. Yet these type of qualities become buried, lost beneath one of the two, in fact, many overarching labels that are affixed. Depending upon one's stance, any interest, venom or admiration just becomes focused around those labels.

Scratch beneath the surface and there is much more to be revealed. Accepting me as a person allows you to see beyond the mist of doubt that may shroud what I do. You may have walked past me on the street or sat next to me on the bus. You didn't develop a highly contagious disease and I didn't assault you or kidnap your kids. I didn't steal your boyfriend or return at midnight to plunder your wife's wardrobe.

And why? Because I am just a normal, run-of-the-mill guy, despite what I may do. Instead of playing football every Saturday, I just happen to indulge in a more unusual, yet harmless activity, should the opportunity arise.

Above all else, I am a father, a husband and a devoted family man. No scandal, no sleaze, no titillation – all rather boring, really.

4–2

Fatherhood

Becoming a father was the best thing that ever happened to me. In many ways, it brought me into line with everybody else. Years of being a social outcast, looking in from the outside and cowering in the corner, were suddenly reversed. The responsibility that was suddenly bestowed upon me, having been carefree for so long, was unbelievable. I could barely look after myself, never mind the tiny, bewildered baby that was suddenly handed to me in the hospital delivery room. As I gazed into my newborn's confused eyes, tears began to well in mine. In finally walking down the same avenue as many others, I was sure to be the toast of the town. My family would be so proud of my achievement.

Emotions were a little mixed on my part because I felt masculine, protective and fatherly; yet, I also felt somewhat inferior and weak because this poor little mite had a cross-dresser as a father. Other babies being born that night would have 'normal fathers'. I really began to question my worth as a man, and even as a person, at this point in my life. All the same, I still had a role and responsibility to play, whereby I wanted to give my child the best start in life – no matter what doubts I had over myself and where I now fitted in society.

With such responsibility, endless nights standing in bars, which for so long had been the mainstay of my single life, were banished into the darkness. Instead, my life was consigned to bags of disposable nappies and cosy, yet sleepless nights in. The thought of propping up a bar, once such familiar territory for me, soon became a distant memory.

As such, I look back on my visits to the nightclubs of Manchester over ten years ago, dressed en femme, with a certain amount of disbelief. Did I really do that? Here I am today, chastising, advising, teaching and trying to teach my child right from wrong. He doesn't know my past, but I do. How credible am I as a role model, having done what I once did?

It all seems a little grubby and seedy now, as I look back. I guess it is because I am much older and wiser. The thought of me sneaking around the back streets of Manchester these days, in women's clothes, makes me shudder. But that is only because I perhaps lack the younger, more daring, adventurous and fun-loving nature I once had. And anyway, being on the street's after two a.m. whilst in male guise is now so unnatural to me. I guess age and responsibility change things pretty quickly – attitudes, perceptions and actions.

There is a flip side to this… What I would also give to have the freedom to do it all again. I am almost envious of my old self! But my new, responsible life and standing give me something I never used to have when locked behind closed doors on my own. Despite less opportunity to dress and the comfort that it brings, I am content in other ways and have interests that once weren't there.

Thinking further, it isn't the thought of me wearing such clothing whilst on the streets that now seems grubby and seedy – not at all. It was the clandestine approach I had to adopt and ensuing guilt that consumed me that tainted those distant but great nights out.

As I grow older, I am more conscious of the need to look after myself. I had quit smoking over ten years prior to Jake's birth. Following several failed attempts, it just miraculously came together one day – clicking into place. Days without a cigarette soon became months, which, in turn, became years. I didn't think

I had it in me. I had foolishly taken up smoking during my teenage rebellious period because I believed I looked hard and cool partaking in such a habit. I thought it would be a bit of a laugh and it would set me a challenge – namely, could I pack it all in again? Whilst I did eventually meet my challenge, the smoking habit had me gripped for a long fifteen years.

With smoking out the way, conquering my addiction to bars would prove much harder. Without the arrival of Jake, I would probably still be in them now, although the ever-increasing price of alcohol may well have started to put me off. Some find going to a gym a way of relaxing following a hard day's work. For me, it was a trip down to my local. Three or four pints at the end of a hard day saw me right. Very often, I would be propping the bar up on my own. In many ways, I didn't mind this because it gave me time to think and analyse situations that had occurred in my life. I would review things that had happened that day, reliving the moment and noting how I could or should have done things differently. But my mind could just as equally have been in neutral; I could merrily gaze at nothing, comfortable in my own little world and minding my own business.

Pubs provided a haven for me whereby I could temporarily numb the pain of my many worries and conflicts. Not that some of the bars I drank in could be classed as a particularly safe haven, but for me, they were the centre of any village life – the heart that kept the village alive. Take the pub out of the equation and the village is a much weaker place. Despite my love for them, the potential for danger, especially in the inner-city areas, was never far away. When I was in my twenties, I used to get challenged a fair bit, usually by men much shorter than me, who felt they had something to prove. It is an inherent fault within many men – never wanting to be seen as being fair game and never wanting to back down against another. I always had the height but was slim in build and therefore was probably looked upon by some as fair game.

In spite of my skinny frame, I was reasonably strong. I once took part in an unofficial arm-wrestling contest in a nightclub and was beating everyone put in front of me – including a real powerhouse who had just stepped out of the gym. I was on the brink of suggesting bets as I was doing so well, but then a doorman broke it all up, telling us to cut it out or leave the club. I surprised myself. I knew I was fairly strong due to lugging bricks around all day, but I didn't realise just how strong I could be. As strong and tall as I was, I was no fighter. I had a soft, caring nature. In many ways, I was a gentle giant, and it took me a long time to get riled.

With my smoking and drinking days behind me, fatherhood brought me a new challenge – what was I to do about my penchant for cross-dressing? How could such a need, indeed a compulsion, fit into my newfound family life? I have often wondered whether I could overcome my need to cross-dress in a similar way to the smoking – i.e. via sheer willpower. But unlike smoking, the same motivation to give it up has never been there. Part of me wants to give my dressing sessions up because I would then have an easier, less stressful life, enabling me to concentrate more on my family. That is counterbalanced, because a large part of me doesn't want to give it up as a result of the immense enjoyment, inner calmness and sense of being that it brings me. That is not a good starting point when wanting to moderate any behaviour. With smoking, I knew that I had to give it up both for the sake of my health and wallet. I knew why I smoked, and how I had come to start. It had been my choice to start smoking fifteen years earlier. It was also my choice to give it all up. As difficult as it was, there was an element of control, despite it being such a powerful drug.

Cross-dressing is different. I am unsure why there is a continuing need for me to indulge in such an activity and unlike smoking, I am not one hundred percent sure of where or when my desires actually started or indeed for what reason. More importantly, my inclination to pack it all in is somewhat half-hearted at best. That is the major difference. It is as though cross-dressing was there from the start, hormonal perhaps, whereas smoking obviously wasn't. I had no say and no decision in whether I became a cross-dresser – it is so deeply entrenched. But it is also what makes me what I am. It makes me tick. It is a major ingredient that contributes to the complex being that is me. If the wearing of female attire increased my chances of suffering cancer or heart disease then my motivation to give it all up would surely rise to a heightened level. But the reality is that wearing female articles of clothing doesn't damage my health. The immediacy of any attempt to pack it all in is therefore not as prominent as it was with the smoking.

I will never be able to totally give up what is such an important part of my life. I accept that. So the next step down is could I moderate my behaviour? It would be ideal if I could limit my dressing to an occasional basis and make it less obsessive and compulsive. But what would I class as being occasional? Once a month? Once every three months? How would I cope in between dressing sessions without the constant, expensive, support of a therapist or other motivator? How would I keep myself occupied, filling the bleak, empty gaps whilst my moments of dressing were put on ice?

"Are we not enough for you?" Donna had once asked me, relating to the fantastic family that I had, yet still having my need to cross-dress.

It was a good question, but clearly asked by someone with a certain amount of naivety in that subject area. It had the ring of a semi-ultimatum. I could be the most powerful man on Earth, I could win the Euro Lottery, have women falling at my feet, but the need to dress would still remain. It is no disrespect to Donna or anyone else around me, but my need to be my true self remains, whatever. It is something that one signs up for when becoming involved with a cross-dresser. Admittedly, it is not necessarily expected that it will be accepted with open arms, but it must at least be tolerated in order for the relationship to stand any chance of surviving. There will always need to be some room for accommodating the feminine side. For the forced purging of dressing to please a loved one could occur for many months, but the inevitable is always just around the corner.

A definite motivation for any attempt at moderation has to be my child. The more I dress, the more I increase my chances of being caught, and as a role model to him, I can't allow that. It is strange that in many ways, I have become part of the 'social problem' myself. In an ironic twist, I am feeding into the stiff-upper-lip, boys-don't-cry type of parent that I despise so much. If my son cries, I am quick to try and stop him. I don't want him to be looked upon as being weak or a cry-baby. I encourage him to play football and partake in karate. I frown when I see him taking an interest in dolls' houses or girly activities and swiftly try and turn his attention to a more boyish activity.

Whilst thinking about colouring my rapidly greying hair recently, I picked up some women's hair dye in a local shop because the women's range had far more choice. As I studied the contents of the box, which included a photograph of a very attractive woman, Jake smiled and innocently asked, "Are you becoming a girl, Daddy?" In a desperate attempt not to influence him with anything unduly feminine, I put the dye back and rebuked, "Don't be silly." I just couldn't let him catch me with my masculine guard down.

How I see it, is that if Jake turned out to be a cross-dresser or gay, then so be it. I would love him all the same. But what I don't want is to believe that I influenced him in any way – no matter how small that influence may have been. I couldn't live with myself if I were guilty of that. Therefore, the situation that I now find myself in is that I feel the need to deter potentially feminine interests displayed by Jake as much as I can. This isn't to be cruel or restrictive; it is because I don't want him to face the same problems, frustrations and fears that I have suffered. I want him to be amongst the majority – being unique and interesting, yes –

but still being amongst the majority. I don't want him sneaking around, lying and constantly afraid of being caught. I want him to have an orderly, loving life in which he can reap the rewards of a healthy and settled lifestyle. That is my dream for him, in any case. I feel that by steering him back onto a path of 'normality', I may hopefully be aiding him to achieve this. I am fully aware, of course, that my actions may have the opposite effect. After all, I don't want to be that overbearing father who turns his son to cross-dressing by not allowing adequate expressions of femininity during childhood.

As such, the situation is confused. I want to lash out with frustration, and it is society with whom I have the problem. It not only dictates how I should behave but is now dictating how I should influence my son to behave, too. I admire those parents who allow their boys to dress freely in girls' clothing as youngsters, though I am not sure I am in total agreement with it. Freedom and being at ease with oneself is great, but if it leaves your child in the firing line, a prime target for ridicule or bullying, then I'm not so sure. And if the class bullies don't get you, you can guarantee the tabloids will succeed later in life – especially if you're in a position of power or responsibility.

4–3

Behaviour Management

If I am to curb my dressing – managing it so that I partake less frequently – I am at a loss as to how I would go about achieving it. How do I bridge the gap between dressing sessions without suffering the dreaded cold turkey? I have previously considered one possibility in the form of clothes substitution – male clothes that achieve a similar image to female clothing. For example, a plain black male cotton vest clings to my body, and with its low neckline has a feminine look. Similarly, plain black men's running bottoms are similar to female leggings. Various unisex ankle pumps could complete the look. It is a possibility, but as mentioned previously, the look alone isn't enough. It is the link with females that gives me comfort. Therefore, women's clothes are what I need – not unisex and certainly not men's. But if these can provide some sort of stop gap, it at least allows me easy access to them. They can be stored in my wardrobe and drawers without fear of being discovered. How I would get around the wig and make-up side of things is another matter, as there is clearly no male substitute for those. But this demonstrates the level of my thinking, scrambling every corner of my mind, frantically seeking the ultimate solution.

Maybe, sacrifice is the only option open to me? That would mean an extravagantly large helping of cold turkey – for life. After all, there are many parents who have been forced to make sacrifices for the sake of their kids before – including putting off separation until their kids have flown the nest. However, as honourable an option as it is, it is not a realistic one. Not now, not ever.

It's a mess, an absolute mess, and my head is in a spin. However, there is nothing new in these thoughts. This isn't new territory for me as it is how I have felt since I was first drawn to female items at thirteen years of age. As I rapidly approach fifty, I still feel the same fears, frustrations and loneliness that I felt over thirty-five years ago. I'm sure these feelings will remain until my dying day, as my compulsion remains clutched around my neck.

I don't wish to come across as constantly moaning because I realise that I have been blessed in life. I was blessed with fantastic parents, a loving family and now with a great wife and child. I love and have loved them all dearly. I have perhaps been plagued with the burden of cross-dressing, yet also been blessed with having the best of both worlds. I have been stupid at times, as well as naïve. I have made countless poor decisions and at times behaved appallingly. But above all this, I am a loving father, trying my best to do the right thing for my family, my community and indeed for the wider environment.

4–4

Missed Opportunities

Talking of poor decisions, I should really have utilised my art school experience more. As I look back, I realise that I was ideally placed. I was at a crossroads in my life. I could continue along the route I was going, which would have been the wrong way, or I could have turned into a new, fresh route. As a result of me taking the wrong route at that juncture of my life, I entered art school with a poor attitude. My days there were fraught with problems from the very beginning. For a start, I couldn't draw very well, nor could I paint. I am perhaps being a little harsh on myself here because like everything else I'd ever attempted, I was probably, at the very least, average, which, thankfully, is somewhat better than hopeless.

In fairness, you didn't have to be good at drawing to do well in art school, though having such a talent obviously helped. Opportunities lay in other areas across a broad artistic spectrum – areas such as pottery, sculpting, photography, film, and, of course, fine art, which, to me, basically involved splattering a load of paint onto a canvas background and wondering if anybody could decipher what it actually was.

The art room was a mass of weird and wonderful structures. Cut-up pieces of material and plastics and rolled-up pieces of paper adorned otherwise dreary, aging walls with life and colour. So long as you were arty and imaginative and could justify what you were doing, you were likely to be fine. Being a bit 'way out' in appearance and therefore interesting also helped of course.

My problem was that I wasn't interested and looked, well, normal. I had struggled through two sittings of O' level exams and whilst I was unlikely to get 'Study King of the Year' award, I felt tired having worked on them. As I saw it, art school would at least allow me to cruise for a few months as the pressure of school had been lifted. That was my hope, in any case.

Unfortunately, it didn't take long for the art school tutors to home in on me. I opted for photography as my intended subject but was only bluffing. I would take a few photos here and there but didn't impress anyone with my works. Time and time again, I would have pencils and paper put in front of me, whereby the tutors tried to make me draw. I would just up and leave, heading out onto the streets with a cine camera or a stills camera, only to return later to feel the full force of the tutors' retribution.

One day, for no particular reason, I drew pictures of some brightly designed neckties. Although I admit it myself, I was quite pleased with them.

"This is a completely different direction for you, Paul," my tutor commented, with more than a hint of hope in her voice.

It didn't last. My brief flirtation with fashion design was over just as soon as it had started. Inevitably, I was asked to leave art school at the end of the spring term. I wasn't too bothered. I was young, carefree and protected by my loving family. I was hardly going to starve as a result of being kicked out, but the humiliation was a little uncomfortable to bear at the time.

But as I look back on those days some thirty years on, I can't help but feel that I missed a golden opportunity. As a young, closeted cross-dresser, I could have utilised my brief migration into fashion and design. I could have immersed myself in a whole world of colour and glamour, designing women's clothing all day, every day. I suppose I could also have designed occasional items for men to make my penchant for things of a feminine nature less obvious to the outside world. I could have designed women's dresses, skirts and hosiery. I could have made shoes from wood and material and decorated them accordingly as part of my portfolio. I could have designed and made a glorious dress for a final project and modelled it myself for photographic purposes. Having made women's clothing as part of my college project, I could then have legitimately stored the items back at home to wear as and when needed, evading the inevitable guilt suffered from wearing my mother's clothing.

I could have experimented with make-up designs – everything from the wacky and bizarre through to the stunningly classy. I could have applied make-up to others – anyone brave or naïve enough to sit before me. I could have had my make-up designs copied onto my own face by a make-up artist for the purposes of photographing them, as a kind of double bluff.

'Sure, he's wearing make-up and women's clothes, but he is surely just putting an artistic twist on it, a different perception, another level to his creation,' others might have said.

The scenario is full of 'what ifs' and remains a definite missed opportunity. However, even if I had thought along those lines and used a bit of cunning to openly immerse myself within the feminine side, reality would still have muscled its way in. I lived with my parents at the time and didn't want them to know about my other side. Any student exhibitions that were put on would have been out there for them to see. I had friends who also attended the course and they could have reported back what I was up to, so therefore my antics and my creativity could have been somewhat stifled.

As such, any of the wacky, out-of-the-closet-type actions may well have had to wait until I was at an art polytechnic, living away from parents and friends. I could have been with others with similar fashion interests who may have accepted me indulging a little on the other side – especially within the realm of my own creations. Even away from home, though, there would still have been the potential for my parents and friends to find out; however, the chances were perhaps a little more limited.

I suppose that if you're 'out' then you have to be one hundred percent out. You can't be half out. As such, the only other route – the one taken by the majority – is to take the clandestine path, where no one can link your feminine image with your usual image.

That is what life is about, making mistakes and missing opportunities, but as a result of missing that particular break, my life was to take a completely different direction – and not necessarily for the best.

I try not to have regrets and try to take as many positives from life as I can. There are people with far worse situations than me – the sick, the needy and disabled being examples. My potential problems in my gender overlap appear somewhat insignificant by comparison. But it is obviously a subject area that I care enough about in order to put it into writing. I am serious about the subject, but can be fun-loving too. I draw the line, however, in circumstances where I have been invited to wear female attire on stag dos and pub crawls. I don't take part because when I do cross-dress, I want to do it properly. I don't want to appear to be on the outside poking fun at something that is such a serious and integral part of me and many others.

If I do have one regret in life, and it is a huge regret, it isn't so much about being born this way or even ending up this way; it is in relation to me not being even closer to my late mother. As close as we were, I feel that my guilt over using her clothes early on in life impeded my ability to get closer, to give her a hug every so often to express my feelings of affection for her. I missed the many chances I had to do such a thing and will never have the chance again. For that, I am forever heartbroken.

4–5

Why?

My thoughts on the subject matter of cross-dressing are different from many others; I accept that. My writing is not from a psychological angle but from a personal one. Nobody knows me better than me, no matter what qualification they may hold. But if others can gain comfort from my words, both in identifying with them and in the realisation that they are not alone, then this has all been worth my time. If I have changed the perceptions of just one person in relation to cross-dressers, especially in a good way, then my time in putting this all together has not been in vain.

In a society that is rapidly advancing towards gender neutrality in certain areas, I can only hope that future generations of cross-dressers don't face the same trials and tribulations that we go through today. After all, a world that allows greater freedom of expression and banishes discrimination, intolerance and bigotry has to be a better world for everyone. But that is all, hopefully, in a better, brighter future. For the moment, I still wake in the middle of the night aghast at what I do. I have physically shaken when, amongst the darkness and the silence of the small hours, the enormity of it all has descended upon me. The realisation that this isn't part of a confused dream that will have dissipated in a few hours leaves me frozen with fear – even over thirty-five years on from my first experimentation with femininity. Something that I thought I had come to terms with and accepted still occasionally creeps up on me, taking me by surprise.

For years, I have tried to understand the deeper motivations that compel me to do what I do. However, the inability to drill down to those thoughts and motivations has created much frustration and uncertainty. Why not play golf, go for a walk or take up painting if I need relaxation? Why does the seemingly bizarre action of wearing a dress create a more relaxed state of mind for me? If it is a transformation that I desire so much, why do I need to transform into a feminine image? Why don't I transform into a different-looking male instead?

It is the exploration of these deeper motivations that may provide some of the much-needed answers to my questions but this is in no way easy. It is as though I can explain ninety percent of my motivation for cross-dressing but the real hub of that motivation lies beyond the permafrost – hidden so deep that it is impossible to get at.

The theories have all been put forward in the past, one of them being an opportunity to escape from the pressures of the male role. Looking at this theory, there is perhaps some merit to it. In not feeling that they can talk as freely about their problems or feelings as women, men can perhaps feel a little isolated. There is a constant pressure to 'man up' or 'grow some' as the modern phraseology goes. The stiff-upper-lip, boys-don't-cry type attitude instilled in youngsters from an early age, certainly doesn't help the cause, either. Ideally, a man should be able to show emotion and, at times, potential weakness, yet still be strong as a result of their better attributes or previous achievements. After all, we all have times when we are fearful, confused or maybe a little lonely.

Having to constantly put on a brave face to fit in with peers and impress women can be somewhat burdensome. There needs to be a pressure release mechanism, whatever form that takes. Talk to my wife, though, and she would tell you that us males have no pressure at all! On a serious note, there has to be a reason behind there being so many suicides amongst young men. I am not suggesting that dressing en femme is the answer to their problems, far from it. The vast majority would not entertain such an idea. However, for some, there may be some merit to the 'escaping from the male role' theory.

Another theory previously put forward is the presence of a dominating father who won't allow any expression of femininity from his son. Whilst my father is old school and believes women – and nobody but women – should be the ones to wear the skirts, he was never overbearing in any shape or form. He showed me nothing but love, support and kindness throughout my childhood and continued throughout my adult life.

There is no doubt that I like the look and the feel of the clothes. I believe women's clothes are better than men's, with more styles, colours and generally more choice. Women's clothes can be sexy and fun. They can be clingy, stretchy and revealing. Men's clothes tend to be duller, heavier and more limited in choice and style. Taking trousers as an example, for many years they were a strictly male-only garment. However, they are a garment upon which women have definitely stamped their own mark. They have been completely rebranded. There are glittery trousers, patterned trousers, fashionably torn trousers, brightly coloured trousers and figure-hugging, sexy trousers from which women can take their pick. A traditional male item has been adopted on practicality grounds and then styled, feminised and marketed into an array of different and attractive fashion options. Sparkly belts and other accessories can add to the overall image. For men, however, there remains mere trousers. Plain old, dull, boring trousers. In the animal kingdom, it is the peacock as opposed the peahen that proudly displays its colours. Alas, in the human species, amongst males, there is restriction and dullness.

If I were to rip and tear my male jeans, dye them pink and coat them with glitter, I would probably be laughed at or possibly worse. Yet they would still be male trousers. They would have been bought from the men's section of a shop. There is, therefore, a boundary, a restriction, to which I have to adhere in order to fit in with my peers. Not only do I have to wear male clothes, but there are restrictions on the styles and colouring that I can wear, too. I am therefore not allowed to be bright, sparkly or pretty. By fitting in with the dress code of the majority, I lessen my chances of assault or ridicule. I can therefore only ever dream of being the 'belle of the ball' for I know it cannot become a reality – not in my lifetime. In a supposedly free-thinking and modern society, I find this very sad. Clearly, this is a highly charged and emotive situation already – and we haven't even started discussing men donning a frock!

It doesn't end there, either. There are more restrictions on how men are supposed to dress even within the drab male fashion world. I have noticed how many men will still have to turn up to the office on a hot summer's day dressed in a suit, a shirt and a tie. Heavy dark leather shoes will adorn their feet. If they are privileged enough, they may be able to ditch their tie at some point in the day. Their female counterparts, however, will wear light strappy sandals, summer skirts and vests. No one bats an eyelid at such inequality in the dress code. It may be true that most men don't have nice feet to look at whilst in sandals; however, how would it be any different if they are expected to wear such heavy shoes in summertime? Similarly, a man who indulges in pedicures may be seen as being a little vain or even effeminate. It's that society attitude thing again.

I once experimented by walking the streets of central London during the daytime wearing a pair of women's black business trousers with my usual male attire. It was only for half an hour or so but it was a very useful experience for me. Examining the trousers closely, you could tell that they were designed for women. For starters, they had no front pockets. They were also designed to be worn without the need for a belt. They were much softer and lighter than men's trousers and far more comfortable. But from a distance, they were less evident as being women's, and I was able to walk the busy streets of London without receiving any strange or disapproving looks.

The satisfaction that was gained by being able to wear an article of female attire in broad daylight was something I had never experienced before. It was the unconscious acceptance displayed by the public that contributed to that satisfaction. I just wished that I could blend in as much and be as 'accepted' whilst wearing a blouse and skirt on those same streets. However, there was an extra satisfaction and naughtiness in me knowing what I was doing, whereas everybody else didn't. It was more challenging than wearing female undergarments under male trousers because obviously, the women's trousers were external and visible to all.

The satisfaction in walking amongst the London crowds visibly dressed in those trousers was interspersed with nervousness about entering shops or crossing in front of stationary traffic. I felt that these were situations in which I could be 'read' or discovered. Looking back, it is strange that I felt so nervous about wearing a pair of black trousers in public. After all, that is what it amounted to – whether they were women's or not – they were merely a pair of plain black trousers. Yet I still felt I could be open to ridicule or worse for wearing, what had until relatively recently, always been considered a male garment.

So why would I gain something from wearing women's trousers and not men's? Again, it is the fact that it is actual female clothing that is the attraction for me. That is, clothing designed for and worn by women. I state this on the following grounds. If I were offered the opportunity to wear satin underwear designed for and worn by women or a very similar set designed for the male cross-dresser, I would opt for the women's underwear. This would be so even though the pair designed for the male figure is likely to fit much better. The problem is that the pair designed for the cross-dresser would just seem too remote and worthless to me.

Why should this be? Why would I turn down the male-designed clothing even though they may have been very similar in style to the women's and may actually be a better fit? I think the reason is that the clothing represents a deep need for identification. It represents a link or a bond that brings me closer with the female gender. Why I need this link or bond lies within the ten percent 'unknown zone' buried beneath my permafrost. Until I can get to the core of that, many of the more testing questions will remain unanswered. On the basis that I have tried to get to the bottom of this for the last thirty years, I don't hold much hope in knowing what makes me tick anytime soon.

What I do know is that I have always admired strong women – women who will take the initiative and make the first move. I also love intelligent and caring, motherly women. I like being looked after and protected by women. I would love to be 'saved' by a woman. As a child, it was Wonder Woman I longed for. I would love to be given the kiss of life by a woman and brought back to life or thrown over the shoulder of a woman firefighter and be rescued from a burning building. To be hoisted from a sinking ship by a woman from a rescue helicopter would be a dream.

Whilst I have come to the aid of a number of people in my time, my role in society appears to be more the damsel in distress than the knight in shining armour. It is perhaps a weakness in my personality, a flaw in my chemical make-up. Whatever it is down to, one thing is certain: I have possessed it since a very young age. Could this all be down to an overbearing or ineffective mother and I therefore crave mothering? Not at all in my case. My mother was an extremely caring, loving type and in no way could she be classed as overbearing or ineffective. She gave me everything I could ever have wanted. She was the best.

I don't think that I have been negatively influenced by my mother any more than other non-cross-dressing males. But by dressing the way I do, I am identifying with my heroines. I am honouring and acknowledging my role model, that is, the female gender. I feel as though I am enveloped in comfort and security when dressed en femme. Like a child longing for the comfort of their security blanket, I get the same comfort from the wearing of women's clothing.

There is, therefore, clearly more to this than the mere clothes themselves. They are a significant ingredient, or means to an end, but it is the need for association with women that I suspect is possibly at my core and the dressing is what quells that particular need or hunger. By both dressing and looking feminine, it at least allows me to become an honorary member of the female community – albeit for brief and infrequent periods of time.

On a more surface and basic level, I am, of course, drawn to the feminine look. It is not enough for me to just wear the clothes themselves – I love make-up and I love the whole transformation. Like many of us, I wish that I had been born better-looking. The application of make-up helps me achieve a better look to a certain extent. Whilst I am no stunner, I do look better, brighter and more colourful when in my female guise. I have always enjoyed the decorating of a Christmas tree – seeing the dark, green branches gradually transformed and brought to life with each application of the fairy lights, tinsel, beads and decorations. Similarly, when applying make-up, the plain foundation base is built upon, and that base gradually becomes the fully decorated article.

I have received many compliments in the past when dressed en femme. I loved that side of things. I love the attention and being prettier than I am allowed to be normally. Whenever there is a wedding, the focus is naturally on the bride, no matter how well turned out the groom may be. On Ladies Day at the Grand National horse race, the Oscars and similar events, the attention is obviously focused upon how well turned out the women are. After all, if it is Ladies Day, then it is their big day, and the attention should rightly be on them. But I crave some of that attention as well and I can't have it, because I am locked in this dull, drab male world. I realise that there is a pressure on women to constantly look good and that brings its own problems for them. Yet I still feel like I am banging on the doors of a prison cell, pleading –

screaming even – to be let out. Cross-dressing, even in private, at least gives me some sort of escape and identification with those types of events. Again, albeit for a short amount of time – and without the need to wear a silly hat!

The thought that I will never taste such freedom to openly be who I really am leaves me depressed and somewhat desperate. Whilst attitudes to cross-dressing and the whole subject of transgenderism appear to have softened over the years, progress is still occurring at a snail's pace. I feel trapped, restricted and claustrophobic. I was born with many feminine qualities within me, and by mixing those qualities with my male attributes, I truly believe that it results in me being a better person. The problem is that those feminine qualities physically need to come to the surface on occasion. And, like a volcano, they eventually erupt in a spectacular and colourful finale. The more my feminine feelings are suppressed, the more unhappy, anxious and restricted I feel. The result of such suppression is the creation of enormous personal stress. After all, I am being denied access to being my true self. The reality is that nobody can deny who they are for too long without feeling some sort of negative effect. I can often be moody and snappy when under such stress.

A sideline to the motivation is also the naughtiness of it all. That has to play a significant role. Like the little child constantly being told not to do something but doing it anyway, I continue to defy the beliefs of wider society.

A question I have asked myself is whether my cross-dressing may be attributed to my lack of success with women. It does have to be said that there was a quiet rebellion going on there somewhere. 'Nobody wants me, nobody likes me – boohoo. Well, just for that I am going to dress in the clothes that society dictates I shouldn't wear.' As laughable as it may sound, perhaps there is some truth in it. But that aside, I strongly believe it is more of a soothing thing. No matter how insulting, nasty, time wasting, testing and rejecting some of the females I've met have been, my female persona would always be there if I needed it – standing in the wings waiting to comfort me as and when required. It has often been suggested that cross-dressing is an escape, and perhaps this was what it was for me. Ironically, it is probably true to say that cross-dressing is only an escape whilst it remains unacceptable to society.

Some ultimate questions remain, for the main part, unanswered, and bleed out into other areas. For instance, why was I always attracted to older women whilst I was younger? Was it a motherly type figure I was after? Did it stem back to my fascination with Jane that day back in my grandmother's living room? Maybe the blueprint does stem back to that time. After all, my interest in feminine clothing was part of my life long before my lack of success with women surfaced.

There was no obvious sexual or other premeditated motive for me to push a toy across Jane's legs that fateful day; that is what four-year-olds do. There are probably millions of youngsters who have pushed toys across their mothers' and aunties' legs in the past and thought nothing of it. With me, it was different. That moment was possibly the moment that influenced me for the rest of my life. I recall Jane saying at the time that she was going to eat me. Looking back, it is the kind of thing you will say to a four-year-old, especially if they are cute enough to eat or to initiate playful 'I'm going to get you' type games. I recall being very disappointed when she didn't carry out her gastronomic threat! I suppose, at four years of age, the thought of being the centre of attention of an attractive, cannibalistic female was quite exciting. Whilst all this may seem trivial banter between an adult and a child, I believe this incident to be most important in understanding why I began to cross-dress.

This is because Jane was bigger than me, stronger and faster than me. She could control my every move if she so wanted. I idolised her, wanted to be her or at least be a part of her. My thinking at the time was that if she *had* eaten me then that would have become possible – I would indeed have been a part of her. The clingy, stretchy clothes that she wore became a significant part of my overall fascination and desire for her.

So is it a domination-type thing, maybe? I'm not necessarily talking whips and chains here, but is it me being weak and lacking alpha-male qualities and seeking strong female support instead?

Whatever the reason, a flickering flame had been ignited that would eventually burn brighter and more ferociously in the years to come. Jane's massive influence on me that day would ensure that I was compelled to emulate it, and her, further on down the line. Obviously, clothes would be a part of that, and just like Jane, black turned out to be my favourite colour. In a similar vein, dark bobbed hairstyles also became my favourite choice when it came to wigs. Looking in the mirror over the years, I became Jane, I became Anna Ford, I became Toyah Willcox – I became all the women, aside from my mother, who have impressed and influenced me along the way.

The early fascination with women's hosiery cannot be ignored. Playing with Jane's legs and noticing the boys in my school playing the reindeer whilst wearing tights are examples of this. The truth is, probably all those boys grew up never wearing a female item again. There is, therefore, much merit in the adage of 'you may cross-dress, but you aren't necessarily a cross-dresser'. As for me, those experiences just happened to either turn me or enhance what was already there. In having actual nylon stockings as Christmas stockings as a child, the whole Christmas experience took on a new and even more exciting dimension.

Running that cool nylon through my fingers on a Christmas Eve surely added to my later interest in wearing such items. Pulling the array of presents and novelties out of that stocking on a Christmas morning allowed me to legitimately feel the softness of the nylon clinging to my hands and lower arms as I did so. In many ways, the excitement of Christmas and seeing long-awaited presents through the micromesh of the nylons became associated with everything that was exciting and magical to me. It acted in a kind of reversed aversion therapy technique. Instead of steering me away from nylons, it, in fact, drew me closer.

It is both strange and disappointing that I remember Jane more vividly in that first memory than any other family member. Closer family members such as my parents and grandparents aren't able to be visualised, though I know they were there. But for whatever reason, I was attracted to Jane. Maybe, just maybe, there was an unconscious sexual attraction towards her even at that tender age? If I was turned on by her image and the clothes whilst being sexually aroused, it possibly created an affiliation at that time. Maybe that led to some sort of chemical or emotional imbalance that would stay with me for a lifetime? It has to have been something that was learned along the way. After all, it wasn't inherited from my father, who is as straight as they come. You can't kid a kidder, and I can spot a fellow trans at a thousand paces.

However, memory is a strange thing. It is sometimes difficult to distinguish between what has actually happened and what you think has happened. This is a fact that I am only too aware of. As I grow older, events that happened a mere six months ago are now distorted. The edges of the memory can become blurred, and what was actually done or said can become misconstrued in a 'Chinese whisper' type of way. The order of events can become mixed up and even people whom you thought were present could actually have been miles away at the time.

An example here is with regards a holiday that I had when I was nine years old. We were in North Wales, and I remember being in awe of a great mountain that faced our holiday cottage. I recall it being beautifully picturesque, Swiss in its nature, and its imposing magnificence greeted us each day as we left our holiday home. Some years later, I went back to find the cottage we had stayed in. I have always been a bit nostalgic in doing things like that. Having found the cottage, the mountain was not as beautiful or as imposing as I had remembered. In fact, it was situated well away from the cottage, at least five or six miles in the distance. It was brown and barren-looking in its appearance and certainly not what you would describe as Swiss-looking.

So if this is the case, what of my first memory? How much of that can now be relied upon? How much credence can be given to that memory as the starting point for my life as a cross-dresser? After all, the Welsh holiday was more recent than my first memory and I still got that gloriously wrong. Whilst the memory can and does fade and images become somewhat distorted, the general facts do remain. After all, the mountain did exist and it was sort of facing the cottage – albeit from at least five miles away. The finer detail had been lost but my memory generally served me well. Similarly, with my earliest memory, the finer detail will be distorted. Gaps may now be filled with assumptions, but the main facts from that memory still remain. Of that, I am ninety-nine percent sure.

4–6

Perversions

One part of cross dressing/transvestism that I have always shied away from talking about is the sexual part because I believe it overshadows the many qualities of the decent cross-dressing community. But it pays to be honest; otherwise, my writing will lack credibility. There *is* something sexually attractive about certain items of women's clothes. I don't think anyone could deny that. A basque, stockings and suspenders are designed to look sexy. Straight men who never cross-dress will, in many instances, be attracted to them and find them a turn-on when worn by their woman. They may want to look at and touch the clothes, feel the sensations of the silks and the nylon – just as I had wanted to do with Sally as a teenager.

But added to the whole sexiness aspect, I feel sure that women themselves also feel sexier and more attractive whilst wearing those items as opposed to wearing jogging bottoms or a duffle coat. Cross-dressers are just an extension of that. They, too, may feel sexier, momentarily leaving behind their grey and stuffy world whilst temporarily shrugging off their restricted image. Looking sexier and more feminine makes me feel more confident than I normally do – even if my 'sexiness' is a figment of my own imagination! Cross-dressers may reflect a favourite female image – the re-enactment of which may be a turn-on in itself. They suddenly have that desired female image there before them, alone and one-to-one. Whilst feminists may want to burn their bras in protest, cross-dressers may merely suggest they pass them on to them instead. It's as simple as that – opposites, differences, variations, it's what makes this big world tick and seem more interesting.

There is, however, a darker, seedier side that can blight the cross-dressing community. This is a side that lets the majority of decent cross-dressers down due to its association with pornography, fetishism or sadomasochism. Whilst I tend to live and let live in most circumstances, the problem I have here is that we all tend to get tarred with the same brush. Society then condemns us as a whole and lashes out in various forms because we are all perceived as being somewhat twisted, dirty and controversial.

Like any other community, the cross-dressing one contains many differing types and personalities. And believe me, I have met or liaised with some real arrogant cross-dressing tossers in my time. But it is easy for us all to be misconstrued because of the activities of a few. I recall a newspaper story about a man breaking into a woman's house while she was out and masturbating into her underwear. It shocked and disgusted me that somebody could do such a thing. To invade her privacy and desecrate her belongings like that is beyond all comprehension.

He probably wasn't a cross-dresser, but the mere fact that women's underwear was involved casts a shadow over the likes of me. It calls into question what I am about and capable of doing. I, too, would be classed as being strange, twisted and perverted. Yet the truth is I am law abiding, caring and sensitive to other people's needs. If a rapist attacked a woman with a cricket bat, cricketers wouldn't get lambasted. It is a similar situation here.

It frustrates me so much that, as a decent person, my type are constantly being put down, feared or treated with hilarity, and unfortunately, incidents such as that one don't help us one bit in our cause for greater acceptance. The perpetrator of that crime wasn't a cross-dresser; he was a burglar and a sexual deviant – two completely different worlds. Having been a victim of a burglary myself in the distant past, I know what it is like to suffer intrusion.

I felt unclean because some faceless criminal had been in my family home and rifled through my belongings. The thought of them taking what they desired without a thought for the feelings of those they were taking from left me cold. Therefore, to have a complete stranger violate your underwear drawer in such a way is beyond all comprehension.

The sexual side of some cross-dressers has also annoyed me immensely in the past. I have previously attempted to find a cross-dressing friend – a straight male with similar morals to me, someone whom I could meet from time to time and, rather than chatting over a drink, we would instead chat about football, DIY or politics whilst dressed. Unfortunately, my attempt to find such a person proved fruitless as all the contact ads were after one thing – sex. The thought of one-night stands with complete strangers repulsed me. Unfortunately, the types of guys I wanted to meet for friendship were probably non-scene, introverted and hidden away like me. They were probably too fearful of reprisals to be that 'out' and by remaining hidden were protecting themselves and their families. The sad fact is, the hidden quiet ones probably represent the majority of the cross-dressing community. The loud, brash overtly sexual ones who tend to be 'out' usually paint a poor picture for the rest of us.

It doesn't help the cause in that cross-dressers have always attracted a certain amount of incorrect or bad press. In many ways, it is hardly surprising. There are many instances where the law-abiding family guy who just happens to dress in female attire is let down by others who involve women's clothing in their crime. Such stories will always hit the headlines, and rightly so.

There are stories such as those that involve men soliciting for the purposes of prostitution whilst wearing women's clothing, or those that involve men stealing women's clothing from washing lines or whilst burgling their victims' dwellings. There are those who sickeningly take articles of clothing as 'trophies' from their victims, having raped or sexually assaulted them first. A tabloid newspaper once ran an article on a killer and provided a picture of him, emblazoned across the front page, dressed in petite articles of women's underclothing. The tiny clothes that stretched across his overly muscular body looked somewhat silly on him. To be honest, as a result of what he'd done, they actually looked repulsive. If the background to this story hadn't been so dark and tragic, the picture would have been somewhat amusing, even to a touchy cross-dresser like me.

The question needs to be asked, though, as to why the paper ran with a picture of him dressed like that as opposed to any other picture? Clearly, they wanted to belittle him and possibly make him look emasculated. After all, a man wearing women's clothes is an easy target, whether you are a murderer, a doctor, a bank clerk or a builder. I feel so frustrated that this should be. I had no problem with the paper trying to tarnish the killer's macho, muscular image but just wish they hadn't used him wearing women's clothes as the tool with which to do so.

It is still strange why men wearing what are traditionally considered women's clothes should be seen as being so derogatory. After all, many women now hold positions of power and lead executive lifestyles. Women, in general, are much stronger and organised as a force than men. Their clothes can and should be seen as symbolic of that power. Yet the comical side will always push to the fore, exacerbated by comic characters such as pantomime dames and Dame Edna. But in depicting a killer dressed like that, it just meant, yet again, that men dressing in women's clothes are portrayed in a bad way.

There is a subliminal message given out that associates cross-dressing with everything seedy and criminal. English citizens had to suffer for a long while with bad press and hostility from their European neighbours as a result of English football hooliganism. The English population as a whole weren't hooligans – far from it. It was, once again, the minority that spoilt it for the majority. But, as with the scenarios mentioned above, the minority who do attract bad press are enough to bring undeserved hardship upon the rest, no matter what compartmentalised band you are in.

One thing I have noticed is that television programme makers will always seek out the more entertaining individuals when it comes to cross-dressers, editing that footage for dramatic and entertaining effect. Thereby, the resultant programme isn't necessarily reflective of all or even most cross-dressers within society. The makers of such programmes don't focus on the guy who goes out every morning and does a decent day's work but then spends a couple of hours a week quietly dressed en femme whilst watching telly or reading a book. That would be far too boring. Instead, they focus on cross-dressing within another theme, such as domination, prostitution or an overly camp gay or drag-queen-type scenario. They will focus on something that has a bit more spice, scandal or entertainment value. I recall seeing American talk shows where over-the-top cross-dressing characters with above-average stories had been invited onto the show. The result, as ever, was always cringeworthy and embarrassing for any cross-dresser of at least average intelligence.

I would never make it onto those types of programmes, even if I wanted to, because as a regular nine-to-five type of guy, I am just too dull. Even adding the spice of my cross-dressing, I am still dull. I would hardly entertain a studio audience, never mind the nation. It is not surprising that such programmes skew the perceptions of the public towards cross-dressers. It makes people think that we are all like that – over the top, potentially seedy and lacking in moral standards.

4–7

Therapy

Strangely, when dressed en femme, it seems so natural to me. I feel like I am floating and at ease with everyone and everything. It is as though I have been female in a previous life and all the sensations, feelings and emotions come flooding back. I, once again, seamlessly slot into place in a seemingly familiar role.

But with the prospect of a new responsible life ahead of me, I felt I had to change. I wanted to curb my compulsion to cross-dress and felt that hypnotherapy may be the key. I was also interested in counselling. I had declared my desires and compulsions to cross-dress to chatline operators in the past but they were unable to offer anything by way of professional help. To attend a counselling session would be completely different. I would be sitting face-to-face, declaring my innermost secrets to a person instead of hiding behind the anonymity of a telephone. This was a daunting prospect, but I had to confess all, especially if there was to be any chance of blue sky at the end of it.

However, the thought of confessing to someone and then potentially bumping into them in the local supermarket was too disturbing to contemplate. As such, I booked a session with a counsellor who was based one hundred miles from where I lived. I was undoubtedly a little excessive in my caution, but that was how I felt at the time. I had two main, yet basic choices when considering my counsellor – I either booked a male therapist or a female one. After two seconds of thought, I opted for a female one. I just couldn't have brought myself to talk to a male counsellor, certainly not about such a personal and sensitive subject. I would have felt disadvantaged, inferior and emasculated amongst one of my own. I identified with females and so a female counsellor was obviously going to be my first choice. The problem was, females would have no hands-on experience of cross-dressing. They wouldn't have experienced the highs, lows and frustrations that I faced on a daily basis. However, equally so, male counsellors wouldn't, either. They would have to be cross-dressers themselves to fully understand the trials and tribulations that I was going through.

Making a two-hundred-mile round trip to receive counselling was never likely to be sustainable, and therefore, after a couple of sessions, I felt unable to continue. However, I was keen to progress in finding a life without the compulsion to cross-dress. As such, I later attended sessions of therapy with a lady called Sheila. She offered a mixture of hypnotherapy and counselling.

I was a little naïve with the hypnotherapy option. I didn't really know what to expect. I thought that by attending a session or two, my life would be automatically transformed. I felt that I would wake up one day and my dressing would all be a distant memory, and I wouldn't miss it at all. I had expectations that it would never darken my thoughts again, and that the flames of desire and compulsion would be extinguished without the potential for further rekindling. I was, of course, completely wrong and not for the first time. There was no magic wand available in all this. This wasn't a fairy tale. It was life at its gritty best. If I had looked into the whole subject of hypnotherapy beforehand, and thought deeply and realistically about what I actually wanted to achieve, then things may have turned out better.

In my defence, I did enquire with Sheila before booking as to whether she thought hypnotherapy may help with cross-dressing. I also asked that if it did help, would I feel as though there was a void in my life once it had gone. Sheila replied that hypnotherapy could help and that there would be no void. Upon hearing this, I was obviously pleased. I suddenly saw a potential key – a pathway to normality. The appointment was made, and a week or so later, I attended my first therapy session with her. The first session was free of charge and was more of a counselling and getting-to-know-each-other session than anything else. I felt very at ease with Sheila. It was amazing how quickly an hour passed when I was chatting with her. There was so much to tell and offload within a short space of time, I could only ever provide an outline of my issue.

"So when you dress, what is it you mean? Do you use large wigs and make-up?" Sheila enquired.

By her questions, I could see her picturing me as some sort of pantomime dame or drag queen. I recalled I had a photo of myself on my mobile telephone. I had taken the photo because I had got my look just right. It only happens occasionally, but whatever had happened, the lighting, the make-up and wig styling had all fallen into place at the time.

"Is that you?" she exclaimed in surprise as I passed her the phone. "You're gorgeous!"

I am sure that I blushed but I was over the moon to hear her say that. My tactic of 'less is more' in the make-up stakes had obviously worked on that day. Men dressing as women have always been seen as comical – blue beards and midnight shadows breaking through thick layers of foundation, bushier eyebrows, heavier-looking faces and awkward stances. Therefore, as a cross-dresser, to get a compliment such as that is a real thrill. To gain that respect in an area that is hard to achieve means a lot and melts the heart somewhat upon receipt. True, Sheila may have just been being complimentary for the sake of it, but I got the impression she was genuinely surprised that the wreck sitting before her could transform as well as I had. That is a major draw for me to do what I do. I just love the transformation.

"So tell me, what is it you want to gain from hypnotherapy?" she enquired.

"I want to be able to give it all up, to put it all behind me," I replied.

Sheila looked confused and somewhat surprised by my revelation.

"I thought that you may just want to understand why you did it. To understand what the driving force behind it was," she said.

This was where I had made the biggest mistake. There was no way hypnotherapy would work in that way for me because I wasn't being realistic in my aims. No matter how much I tried to convince myself to the contrary, there was no way that I wanted to give it all up. I had made a flippant, throwaway remark and was somewhat reckless in doing so. Since that session, I have read another hypnotherapist's blog who said that if he is approached by someone who wants to give something up, he will always ask, 'How much do you want to give it up? What percentage of you wants to give it up?' Anything less than one hundred percent would mean that the potential client is not ready for that type of therapy. If I had been asked what percentage of me wanted to give the dressing up, I would probably have admitted to a figure of no more than twenty percent, if that.

I enjoyed my hypnotherapy sessions with Sheila. One problem was that she had two teenage kids at home. I had met them as I was entering the house one day. At times, I could hear them banging and clattering upstairs during my session. Sheila would tell me, whilst I was hypnotised, to ignore any background noise and put it to the far corners of my mind. At one stage, she had to leave the room, and although I didn't hear her, I am sure she gave them a good telling-off whilst upstairs. It was all a little too distracting, if I'm honest.

A common mistake when talking about hypnotherapy is to believe that you are put into a trance. It conjures up visions of stage hypnotherapists getting members of the audience to do ridiculous things in the name of entertainment. The reality is that it is not like that at all. You are very aware of what is going on around you, and you are totally in control of what you are doing. You are merely put into a very relaxed state of mind and body. The whole process began by counting backwards and imagining I was walking down steps into a beautiful garden, as well as the relaxation of key muscles within the head and body. Words such as 'you are relaxing deeper…and deeper…and deeper' sent me into a state whereby I felt as though I was slowly slipping – indeed pouring – off my seat like a flattened cartoon character. I relaxed so much that I could not feel my hands and they developed a mild sense of pins and needles. Much of the session was regression, whereby I would be taken back to my childhood to become acquainted with my thoughts and feelings of yesteryear, attempting to pinpoint where my issue had started.

The one striking point I vividly recall was being in a state of mind whereby I was taken back to my grandmother's house. Bearing in mind that I had not been there for some years since her death, I was still able to recollect vividly the distinguishable and pleasant smell of her spare bedroom. It was so clear, and I felt that I had been placed back in time into that room. Despite my eyes being closed, I could see the bed, the cabinet and the sun streaming through my grandmother's window. I have never been able to regain that sense of smell or feeling of familiarity when out of those sessions.

At the end of my first proper hypnotherapy session, I was brought out of my relaxed state to find that the room had very much darkened. It was a late-autumn afternoon. An hour had passed but it only seemed like ten minutes or so. Even in my woken state, I felt so relaxed, as though I had slept for a couple of hours and had awoken to a massage. Driving home, I was more courteous than usual, more patient and more content.

I felt strong enough from that first session not to cross-dress. It felt as though the pain of the desires, the inclinations and compulsions had been subdued and indeed lifted. I felt that Sheila was a crutch upon which I could lean – as though she was my saviour. I now had a self-set target in my own mind, but I had to take things one step at a time. I set myself the goal of not wearing an item of women's clothing until my next hypnotherapy session. Usually, such a thought would send me into a blind panic, so setting a target of a few weeks without wearing anything feminine was quite a challenge for me. In any case, the weeks passed and I attended my next therapy session. I had done it. I had achieved my goal and actually achieved it with relative ease. I couldn't wait to tell Sheila of my success and how much of an assistance her session had been. I was like the class swot who can't wait to take the teacher her rosy-red apple.

Following each session, I would be provided with a CD to listen to. This was for the purpose of self-hypnosis, to energise and become a stronger person within, the problem being that I didn't get much time to listen to the CDs between therapy sessions. There were always distractions of one sort or another. Sheila suggested that I substitute the more 'intimate' female items that I wore for something else. She suggested wearing a pair of women's gloves instead of dressing fully. This replacement hardly inspired me but I was willing to give anything a try. She also advised that it may be a case of attempting to manage my issue as opposed giving it up totally.

With a self-imposed embargo on all things feminine, save for a pair of women's leather gloves, I was actually much calmer than expected. I felt stronger knowing that Sheila was there waiting in the background. On the odd occasion when the compulsion began to bite, I would wear the gloves. It was like trying to warm a room with a candle, but the small amount of affiliation to females through wearing the gloves at least gave me some comfort.

In the end, I only attended four sessions with Sheila. I actually expected the therapy to go on for far longer than that, especially as this was such a deep and complex issue. Indeed, I attended my final session not knowing that it was to be my last. As my fourth session drew to a close, Sheila stated, "Well, that is it, I wish you well. You know where I am if you need me."

I was stunned. Sure, I had told her that I felt stronger and more in control, but I hadn't prepared my mind for this being the last session. I was unsure if I had misled Sheila. Had I come across as being too positive? If I did, the truth was that I still felt vulnerable and weak. I felt as though I were a child learning to ride a bike with a parent holding onto the seat, steadying and supporting my balance. Then, without warning, the parent removed their grip and I was suddenly on my own with a sense of panic setting in. I didn't feel I could tell Sheila that I wasn't ready. I felt she may take it badly – being a reflection on her not succeeding within her own time limits. Sheila should have discussed how I was feeling ahead of the last session. She should have assessed my strength and ability to cope with the situation.

Driving home from therapy that night, I felt alone and unsupported. In fact, I felt let down and abandoned. If pressed further, I would have admitted to even feeling a certain amount of resentment towards Sheila. I had a mischievous voice in my mind saying, 'She has let you down, left you on your own. Go on, start dressing again.'

Admittedly, Sheila could have done things differently, but I also had to shoulder some of the responsibility. By not listening to the CDs outside of my sessions, I had perhaps let myself down. My aims and expectations had also been too high and unrealistic. There was no way I was going to be able to give the dressing up. What I actually needed was to understand and control the situation more. I needed to know what my motivations were and manage those feelings in a controlled way. That was never achieved.

I went three months without wearing any female items whilst attending Sheila's sessions. That was a real achievement for me, and it had to be down to the hypnotherapy. However, with the abrupt end to the sessions, and with me feeling so let down, it was inevitable that my resistance would collapse and I again began cross-dressing with a vigour. I was making up for lost time. Whilst, ultimately, hypnotherapy didn't work for me in the longer term, it is a practice that I still have a lot of time and respect for. I would undertake it again but would certainly have to go in with a different attitude and have clearer, more achievable goals.

As it happens, I haven't returned to hypnotherapy, but I have attended further counselling on an occasional basis as I find it does help to talk and get opinions and ideas from a different angle. During one session, I was asked to think about what my living accommodation would look like when in male guise and when in female. I thought long and hard about this and thought that surely there would be two extremes – the female accommodation would be totally different from the male. This couldn't have been further from the truth.

I concentrated on two rooms – the living room and the bedroom. I used an old catalogue to cut out the objects and designs that I would go for. The lounge was modern, with glass table tops and black leather suites with grey and blue walls. There was a definite hint of bachelor pad there. The bedroom, however, was girly, with pinks, fairy lights and flowery paintings.

So, whereas I thought there would be two definite opposites – a feminine lounge and bedroom for my female persona and a masculine lounge and bedroom for the male, I was wrong. The two were mixed. I could happily live in a functional bachelor pad with a girly bedroom adorned with satins, beads and colour. This seemed strange to me but thinking about it again, why should it be? After all, I am one person made up of two sides – feminine and masculine. When red and white are mixed together, the common ground is pink. And that is me.

Looking at the results, there is no definite separation. I would be unhappy to live in a totally masculine dwelling, devoid of feminine touches, but similarly, would be uncomfortable with over-the-top campness and femininity. Too many pink cushions and curtains would drive me crazy. But mixing the two, albeit via separate rooms, suited my personality. It was a very useful exercise, which effectively demonstrated that both sides of my character cannot be totally separated.

I am amazed that more cross-dressers don't seek out some sort of counselling. Maybe they see it as a weakness or some kind of admission that they have a problem? When I went to see Sheila, she was living on the outskirts of Manchester, a city with suburbs that house over two million people. Taking in other surrounding areas, she was probably sitting amongst a potential three million people. If, for the purpose of example, we say that one in a hundred men cross-dress, then that meant an incredible 30,000 cross-dressers were practically on her doorstep. If one in twenty dressed, that figure would be more like 150,000!

Yet, apart from me, no other cross-dresser had ever visited her. Again, the potential fear and concerns of being outed are probably too much for many to bear. All I can say is that with the right therapist, there could be much benefit to those who feel burdened and pressured by their situation. For me, it wasn't about believing I was weak or had a problem. It was about talking freely to someone who would take an interest in me and my situation. To constantly bottle things up created stress. To talk to a non-judgemental therapist offered a release to that stress. Therapists helped me explore my inner self and actually discover more about me. Sometimes, hearing what you already know but from a different person is an immense help – and I will take all I can in an attempt to understand more about my 'hidden ten percent'.

4–8

Time For a Little Controversy

I despair when I hear cross-dressers calling themselves a femme name like Candy, Bianca, Marcia etc. That, for me, is the real crazy bit. It is the bit that in my mind lets every transvestite and cross-dresser down worldwide. Why? Because you are attempting to adopt a different identity. You are trying to be accepted as being someone else. Introducing a 'third person' to a marriage or partnership can only prove problematic in the long run. How is a wife expected to act when she suddenly has to share her man with 'Gloria'?

If, however, the partnership remains a partnership, with no third person and an occasional bit of dressing, then who knows? I strongly believe it is better to be yourself when cross-dressed. Yes, certain things may naturally change – I apparently become more relaxed and confident when dressed en femme. The key thing here, though, is that it isn't forced by me. Any personality or behavioural change is purely natural due to the change in my image. Beneath the clothes and the make-up, I am still me, Paul. However, if a six-foot-four powerhouse wants to be called Shirley on the occasions he transforms, it will just invite ridicule and make the whole community laughable.

It's a controversial point, I know, but a valid one that rings true in my mind. Eddie Izzard, Danny La Rue, Julian Clary and Boy George have all camped it up to varying degrees over the years but have never felt compelled to call themselves Crystal, Chardonnay or Mimi to reflect their end image. They kept a masculine name, and as such, I believe they were respected all the more for it.

Where a man is totally uncomfortable in himself and seeks gender reassignment, then choosing a femme name is expected, on the basis that they intend to transition to that person one hundred percent of the time. In my mind, it is about only ever being one character – no matter what your image may be at the time. I appreciate not everyone will agree with my view, but I truly believe it is the way forward to greater acceptance.

The problem is that most women want their man to be a man – a 'proper man'. Just what exactly a proper man is, I couldn't tell you. What I do know is that I provide money to buy food, pay for a mortgage and I would fight to the death to protect my wife and son. But am I what society would class as a proper man? I am clean and try to do my bit – tidying the house, cooking a meal every so often, washing the dishes, vacuuming the carpets, gardening, recycling, and bathing Jake. Yet despite these better qualities, I would still be criticised because of my desire to be a little feminine at times. Whilst I may not be considered a 'proper man' by many, I truly believe that I am a good man.

I see how some 'proper men' behave on a daily basis. Selfish, ill-mannered, aggressive, unclean, opinionated and greedy. I wouldn't want to be like that. I would rather be me with all my interpreted flaws. Donna is reasonably broad-minded and has an array of strange and wonderful friends, some of whom are gay, some of whom are plain bizarre. But for her guy to be less than one hundred percent straight is somewhat unpalatable. I think, if we are being honest, this scenario is true of most women. They are probably more tolerant of gays and cross-dressers than most men. They possibly don't see them as a threat and may even view them as being mysterious and interesting. Live and let live – just so long as their own guy isn't like that.

I can't blame women for their general non-acceptance. After all, they have been brought up in the same bigoted and selfish society that we all have. Plus, I have to see things from another angle. How would I take it if my wife told me that she liked wearing men's Y-fronts instead of lingerie? Surely there would be a certain amount of shock there for me? Would it also perhaps be a little amusing? I may even be a little confused and angry because I would prefer her to look and dress like a woman in the stereotypical way. A 'proper woman'. A woman who preferred more silk and satin as opposed heavy cotton. Maybe this would be true, but I hope I would accept her for what she was, whatever her choice.

It is more acceptable in society for a woman to take items of her male partner's clothing. But why should this be? Why can't it be the same the other way round? I think the major difference is that women will wear men's clothing styles for practical reasons. An example here is policewomen. As their roles within the police became more and more frontline, it became impracticable to vault walls in a skirt. Thereby came the addition of trousers to their uniform. Cross-dressers, on the other hand, may wear clothes of the opposite sex for an array of differing reasons, which would include, in my case, psychological benefits. However, if men wear female items for practical reasons – such as tights for leg warmth on a freezing day – they would still fear being caught wearing them. The practicality excuse therefore doesn't extend both ways within this society.

Overall, I am seeking freedom. My ideal is that I could wear my hair long, dye it vivid colours, wear make-up and feminine clothes, and still be called 'sir' without it being used in a derogatory 'I've read you' kind of way. I wouldn't call myself Doris and take on another persona, it would be me – just me – being a father and playing football with my son. But as I say, that is the ideal – for me, at least. A problem is, many men don't look after their appearance and this can lead to intolerance of those who do. Even when in male guise, to have your teeth whitened or have a spray tan can lead to you being the brunt of jokes and negativity from both males and females alike.

AND FINALLY...

So there you have it, my attempt to explain one of the most misunderstood areas of behaviour demonstrated by an unknown, but believed small percentage of males.

Whilst the reasons given are personal to me, I hope that others may also identify with some of the points put forward. I am no doctor, nor am I a psychiatrist, but what I offer is the truth from within my own heart and mind. It is only by offering such truths that one can begin to piece together the motivations and compulsions behind cross-dressing – in the hope they then equate to something understandable.

Unfortunately, the understanding, as hard as it is, is potentially the easier part. It is what is then done with that information and how it can be acted upon that probably provides the greatest challenge of all.

As for me, I am content, I am in control, I am enjoying life – despite its many uncertainties.

However, one thing of which I am totally sure is that beneath the wig, the make-up and the vast array of designer frocks that have adorned me over the years, I will truly and eternally remain, just your average guy.

About the Author

Paul Jason explores the roller coaster of emotions experienced in identifying with both genders. The conflicts, the breakdowns and the traumas – Paul has experienced it all.

Whilst Just Your Average Guy focuses upon this subject matter, it was written with the intention of it appealing to a readership well beyond the LGBT community – to include women, trans admirers and anybody else with a general interest in gender crossover.

Although there are many transgender books available, Paul approaches the subject from a different angle – that of a closeted, 9 to 5, family guy, attempting to balance the straight with the trans whilst encountering all the frustrations in between.

Having written his first memoir, his attention is now firmly focused upon writing fictional stories with a transgender theme.

Beaten Track Publishing

For more titles from Beaten Track Publishing,
please visit our website:

http://www.beatentrackpublishing.com

Thanks for reading!

CPSIA information can be obtained
at www.ICGtesting.com
Printed in the USA
LVOW11s1011181017
552871LV00001B/11/P